SUMMER BRAIN QUEST

Dear Parent,

At Brain Quest, we believe learning should be an adventure—a *quest* for knowledge. Our mission has always been to guide children on that quest, to keep them excited, motivated, and curious, and to give them the confidence they need to do well in school. Now, we're extending the quest to summer vacation! Meet SUMMER BRAIN QUEST: It's a workbook. It's a game. It's an outdoor adventure. And it's going to stop summer slide!

Research shows that if kids take a break from learning all summer, they can lose up to three months' worth of knowledge from the previous grade. So we set out to create a one-of-a-kind workbook experience that delivers personalized learning for every kind of kid. Personalized learning is an educational method where exercises are tailored to each child's strengths, needs, and interests. Our goal was to empower kids to have a voice in what and how they learned during the summer, while ensuring they get enough practice with the fundamentals. The result: SUMMER BRAIN QUEST—a complete interactive program that is easy to use and designed to engage each unique kid all summer long.

So how does it work? Each SUMMER BRAIN QUEST WORKBOOK includes a pullout tri-fold map that functions as a game board, progress chart, and personalized learning system. Our map shows different routes that correspond to over 100 pages of curriculum-based exercises and 8 outdoor learning experiences. The variety of routes enables kids to choose different topics and activities while guaranteeing practice in weaker skills. We've also included over 150 stickers to mark progress, incentivize challenging exercises, and celebrate accomplishments. As kids complete activities and earn stickers, they can put them wherever they like on the map, so each child's map is truly unique—just like your kid. To top it all off, we included a Summer Brainiac Award to mark your child's successful completion of his or her quest. SUMMER BRAIN QUEST guides kids so they feel supported, and it offers positive feedback and builds confidence by showing kids how far they've come and just how much they've learned.

Each SUMMER BRAIN QUEST WORKBOOK has been created in consultation with an award-winning teacher specializing in that grade. We cover the core competencies of reading, writing, and math, as well as the essentials of social studies and science. We ensure that our exercises are aligned to Common Core State Standards, Next Generation Science Standards, and state social studies standards.

Loved by kids and adored by teachers, Brain Quest is America's #1 educational bestseller and has been an important bridge to the classroom for millions of children. SUMMER BRAIN QUEST is an effective new tool for parents, homeschoolers, tutors, and teachers alike to stop summer slide. By providing fun, personalized, and meaningful educational materials, our mission is to help ALL kids keep their skills ALL summer long. Most of all, we want kids to know:

It's your summer. It's your workbook. It's your learning adventure.

—The editors of Brain Quest

This book belongs to:

Nitzan Livneh

Library of Congress Cataloging-in-Publication Data is available.

ISBN 978-0-7611-9328-9

Summer Series Concept by Nathalie Le Du, Daniel Nayeri, Tim Hall
Writers   Bridget Heos, Claire Piddock
Consulting Editor   Kim Tredick
Art Director   Colleen AF Venable
Cover, Map, Sticker, and Additional Character Illustrator   Edison Yan
Illustrator   Carey Pietsch
Series Designer   Tim Hall
Designers   Abby Dening, Carolyn Bahar
Editor   Nathalie Le Du
Production Editor   Jessica Rozler
Production Manager   Julie Primavera

Workman books are available at special discounts when purchased in bulk for premiums and sales promotions as well as for fund-raising or educational use. Special editions or book excerpts can also be created to specification. For details, contact the Special Sales Director at the address below, or send an email to specialmarkets@workman.com.

DISCLAIMER
The publisher and authors disclaim responsibility for any loss, injury, or damages caused as a result of any of the instructions described in this book.

Workman Publishing Co., Inc.
225 Varick Street
New York, NY 10014-4381
workman.com

BRAIN QUEST, IT'S FUN TO BE SMART!, and WORKMAN are registered trademarks of Workman Publishing Co., Inc.

Printed in China
First printing March 2017

10 9 8 7 6 5

SUMMER BRAIN QUEST®

BETWEEN GRADES 5&6

For adventurers ages 10–11

Written by Bridget Heos and Claire Piddock
Consulting Editor: Kim Tredick

WORKMAN PUBLISHING
NEW YORK

4 Contents

Instructions. 5

Level 1. 9

Level 2. 17

Level 3. 29

Level 4A 44

Level 4B 56

Level 5A 74

Level 5B 62

Level 5C 86

Level 6. 94

Level 7. 110

Summer Brainiac Award!. 128

Outside Quests. 129

Key Quests. 134

Answer Key 136

Summer Brain Quest Reading List 145

Summer Brain Quest Mini Deck. 155

SUMMER BRAIN QUEST

Your Quest

Your quest is to sticker as many paths on the map as possible and reach the final destination by the end of summer to become an official Summer Brainiac.

Basic Components

Summer progress map

100+ pages of quest exercises

100+ quest stickers

8 Outside Quests

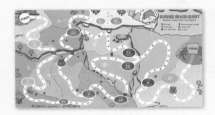

8 Outside Quest stickers

4 Key Quest stickers

Over 30 achievement stickers

Summer Brainiac Award

Summer Brainiac Award

Presented to

for successfully completing the learning journey in
SUMMER BRAIN QUEST®: BETWEEN GRADES 5&6

100% sticker

Setup

Detach the map and place it on a flat surface.

Begin at **START** on your map.

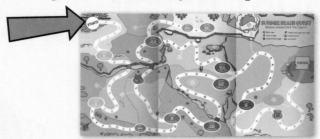

How to Play

To advance along a path, you must complete a quest exercise with the matching color and symbol. For example:

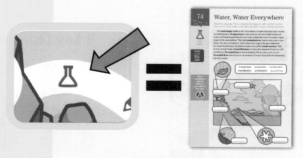

**Math exercise from
the orange level
(Level 2)**

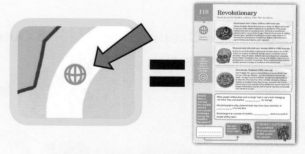

**English language arts exercise
from the red level
(Level 3)**

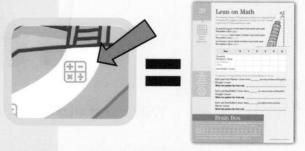

**Science exercise
from the blue level
(Level 5A)**

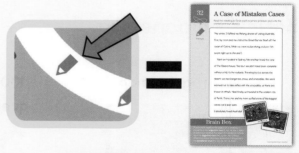

**Social studies exercise
from the green level
(Level 7)**

If you complete the challenge,
you earn a matching quest
sticker.

Place the quest sticker on
the path to continue on
your journey.

At the end of each leg of your journey, you earn an achievement sticker.

Apply it to the map and move on to the next level!

Forks in Your Path

When you reach a fork in your path, you can choose which direction to take. However, each level must be completed in its entirety. For example, you cannot lay two quest stickers down on Level 5A and then switch to Level 5B.

If you complete one level, you can return to the fork in the path and complete the other level.

Outside Quests and Key Quests

Throughout the map, you will encounter paths that lead to Outside Quests and Key Quests. To earn a sticker and advance along those paths, you must complete one of the Outside Quests or Key Quests.

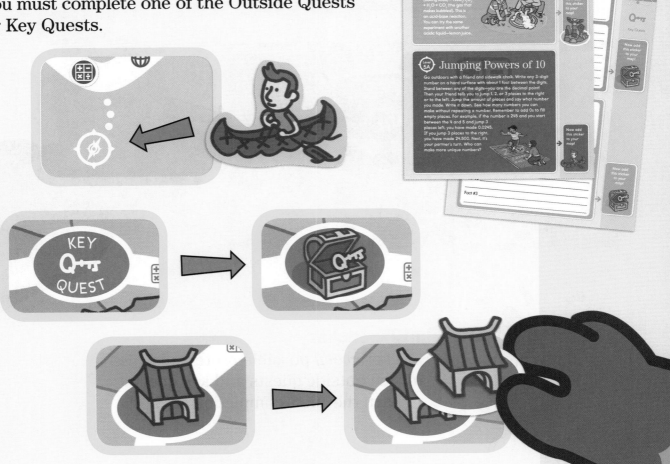

Bonuses

If you complete a bonus question, you earn an achievement sticker.

> BONUS: Complete the sentence: As a cobra's mass increases, it will need to use more _____ to strike at its prey.

→

Now add this sticker to your map!

Subject Completion

If you complete all of the quest exercises in a subject (math, English language arts, science, or social studies), you earn an achievement sticker.

CONGRATULATIONS!
You completed all of your math quests! You earned:

Summer Brainiac Award

Presented to:

_____
for successfully completing the learning journey in
SUMMER BRAIN QUEST®: BETWEEN GRADES 5&6

Summer Brain Quest Completion Sticker and Award

If you complete your quest, you earn a Summer Brain Quest completion sticker and award!

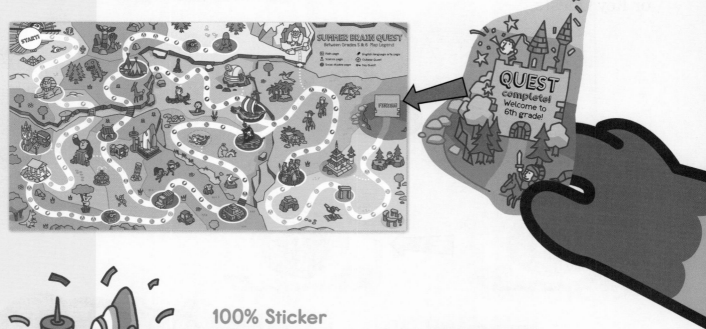

100% Sticker

Sticker *every* possible route and finish *all* the outside quests and key quests to earn the 100% completion sticker!

Level
1

Conjunctions,
Prepositions,
and
Interjections

Upon
completion,
add this
sticker to
your path on
the map!

Giza or Bust

Read the story. Then write C over the conjunctions, P over the prepositions, and I over the interjections.

Yesterday, my sister and I reached Giza. Hurray! We are now pyramid builders. Our job is to move stone blocks from the bottom of the ramp to the top, all to honor our great pharaoh! Our task is simple, but it's neither easy nor foolproof. During the heat of the afternoon, another team lost its grip on a block. The block rolled over a worker's arm, crushing it. Horrible! Doctors came immediately, thank Ra!

By the end of the day, my sister and I were famished. Back home, we are used to small portions of rice and fish at mealtime. Imagine our surprise when heaping plates of pork, goat, and mutton were passed around the table. Yum! After dinner, I tried listening to my new friends' stories, but I couldn't keep my eyes open. Instead, I fell asleep on the hard ground under the stars.

Brain Box

Prepositions show how nouns relate to other words in a sentence.
A **prepositional phrase** often answers the questions **when**, **where**, or **what**.

Example: We walked **through** the village. Where? **Through** the village.

Interjections are words of excitement, command, or protest.
Examples: **Stop**! That pyramid is off limits.
Yay, we outran the mummy!

The Nile

Read about Egyptian civilization developing along the Nile. Then draw arrows from illustration to illustration to show cause and effect. (HINT: There may be more than one cause or effect for each item.)

The Nile

People have always needed water to survive. They need it for drinking, of course, but also to nourish the plants and animals upon which they rely for food. People began settling along the Nile River in the Sahara Desert around 6000 BCE. The Nile flooded each year, leaving behind rich soil for planting. The crops were plentiful, and the population grew. To control the water, people dug canals to provide year-round irrigation for their fields. To keep track of the agricultural seasons, the people created a calendar using paper made from papyrus—a river plant.

The Nile provided food, but the desert offered a gift of its own. Would-be intruders couldn't survive the trek across it. Egypt was safe from invasion. With the basic needs of food and safety met, some Egyptians could turn to other pursuits, such as art, architecture, government, and religion, all of which led to the building of the great pyramids.

Upon completion, add this sticker to your path on the map!

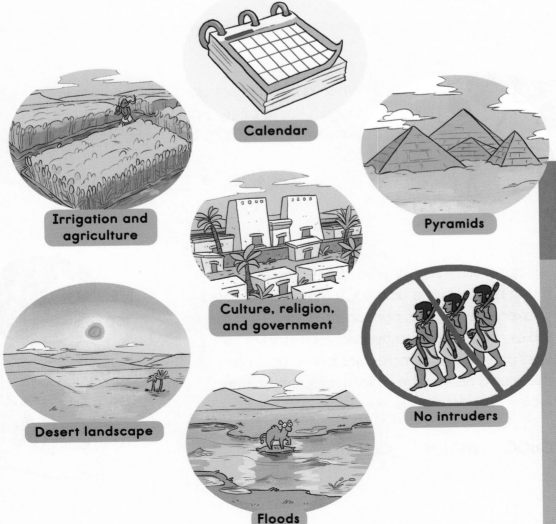

Calendar

Irrigation and agriculture

Pyramids

Culture, religion, and government

Desert landscape

No intruders

Floods

Brain Box

A **civilization** is a way of life that includes culture, specialized jobs, social hierarchy, cities, government, religion, technology, and record-keeping. Historically, civilizations have often developed along rivers, such as Mesopotamia, the Yellow River valley, and the Indus River valley.

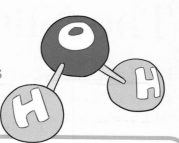

Reaction Action

Read the passage. Then fill in the missing symbols to complete each chemical reaction equation.

Matter and Interactions

An atom is the basic unit of an element. In an equation, each elemental symbol represents one atom. For example, H represents one hydrogen atom and O represents one oxygen atom. Atoms can bond to form molecules. In an equation, H_2 represents a molecule consisting of two hydrogen atoms, called dihydrogen. Similarly, O_2 represents a molecule consisting of two oxygen atoms, called dioxide.

Certain types of molecules react. When the molecules come into contact with one another, they break up and the atoms then rearrange themselves to form new molecules. However, the total number of each type of atom stays the same. For example, the equation $2H_2 + O_2 \rightarrow 2H_2O$ shows that two dihydrogen molecules reacted with one dioxide molecule to form two dihydrogen oxide molecules—also known as water! But the number of atoms (four hydrogen and two oxygen) stayed the same.

When a cow passes gas (CH_4), it reacts with oxygen in the air (O_2) and forms another gas, carbon dioxide (CO_2), and water vapor (H_2O).

$$CH_4 + 2O_2 \rightarrow \_\_O_2 + 2H_2O$$

An upset stomach may be caused by too much hydrochloric acid (HCl). When an antacid is taken, the calcium carbonate ($CaCO_3$) in the tablet reacts with the hydrochloric acid in the stomach. The acid molecules break up, and the atoms rearrange to form calcium chloride, water, carbon dioxide—and stomach relief.

$$CaCO_3 + 2HCl \rightarrow \_\_Cl_2 + H_2\_\_ + CO_2$$

Upon completion, add this sticker to your path on the map!

Millions of Stars

Campers count stars aloud. Write the words as numbers.

Four million three hundred twenty-six thousand, one hundred eighty-five
_4,326,185_

Three hundred twenty-nine thousand, six hundred eight
_329,608_

Seven million seven thousand seventy
_7,007,70_

Sixty thousand eight hundred ninety-four
_60,894_

Campers time shooting stars in seconds. Write the words as decimals.

Six hundred fifty-nine thousandths
_0.659_

Five and four hundred sixty-three thousandths
_5.463_

One and seven hundredths
_1.7_

Seventeen and eighty-eight thousandths
_17.088_

Place Value

Brain Box

millions	hundred thousands	ten thousands	thousands	hundreds	tens	ones	decimal point "and"	tenths	hundredths	thousandths
6	3	7	5	3	7	9	.	5		
						0	.	9	8	7

Mr. Perfect

Fill in the blanks with the correct perfect tense verbs from the box.

had escaped	have asked	will have returned	have studied
had taken	have wanted	hadn't brought	had created

Perfect Tenses

Upon completion, add this sticker to your path on the map!

PADRAIC PERFECT

As many of you know, I ___have studied___ the Great Pyramid of Giza since I was a toddler first learning to read. Naturally, I ___have wanted___ to visit Egypt for many years. This summer, I did just that. My goal was to measure the pyramid to determine how perfect it was mathematically. I ___hadn't brought___ a tape measure, of course. Rather, I ___had created___ an app that allowed me to take measurements based on cell phone photos. I ___had taken___ just a few measurements when my work was interrupted. A mummy ___had escaped___ from the pyramid and refused to leave me alone. Many people ___have asked___ if I took a photo of the mummy. I did not. I was there to measure the pyramid, not take photos of mummies. My only hope is that by next year, I ___will have returned___ to Egypt and completed my work.

BONUS: Write a sentence from the mummy's point of view. Include a past, present, or future perfect tense verb.

One day I was there. A pyramid. I made it my home. Then I see a man. I decide to talk to him.

Brain Box

Present perfect shows that something occurred at an indefinite time or is still occurring.
Example: I **have watched** people loot my tomb since I was first laid to rest.

Past perfect shows that something happened before another past action.
Example: The tomb raider **had escaped** by the time police arrived.

Future perfect shows that an action will occur before another action.
Example: This time next year, I **will have** stopped the looting once and for all.

Now add this sticker to your map!

Energy of the Sphinx

Look at each picture and read the description. Write whether the item has <u>kinetic</u> energy, <u>potential</u> energy, or both.

energy in vse had

A sphinx darts across the desert.

Kinetic

A camel stands on the hot sand.

Potential

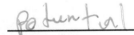

An olive branch rustles in the wind.

Kinetic

Upon completion, add this sticker to your path on the map!

A car weaves through the Cairo traffic.

Potential

BEEP! BEEP BEEP!!
HONNNNNK!!

Brain Box

A hammer is held over a rock.

Potential

Kinetic energy is the energy an object has due to its motion. Example: a runner running a race. **Potential energy** is the energy an object has due to factors that could set it in motion. Example: a runner waiting at the starting line.

Dollars and Sense

Round each decimal number according to the directions.

Rounding
Decimals

23.165 is:

_20,165_ to the nearest ten   _23_ to the nearest whole number

_23,170_ to the nearest tenth   _23,200_ to the nearest hundredth

Round each souvenir price according to the directions.

$8.74 to the nearest whole dollar is _9.00$_
but to the nearest ten dollars is _10 $_ .

$38.49 to the nearest ten dollars is _40 $_
but to the nearest tenth (ten cents) is _38.5¢_ .

$17.45 to the nearest ten dollars is _20$_
but to the nearest whole dollar is _$18_ .

$1.83 to the nearest tenth is _1.80_ .

$5.78 to the nearest tenth is _$5.86_ .

BONUS: A cactus figurine costs $6.49. If the shopkeeper priced it to the nearest hundredth, what numbers could she have rounded?

_$6_   _6.50$_

_____   _____

_____   _____

_____   _____

_____   _____

Now add this sticker to your map!

Level 1 complete!

Add this achievement sticker
to your path...

...and move on to

Level 2!

Be the Archaeologist

Read about the Harappan civilization. Then draw a line to match each artifact to the correct conclusion.

Ancient
Civilizations

Upon
completion,
add this
sticker to
your path on
the map!

Around 4,600 years ago, the ancient Harappan civilization flourished along the Indus River. Its cities were well-engineered, with streets laid out in a geometrical grid, and homes and buildings built of uniform-size bricks. Wells provided water into homes and public baths, and dirty water flowed out through a sewage system. There was a thriving economy, with merchants using unique seals on their products to signify their "brand names." But what sets the Harappan civilization apart from other ancient civilizations is its apparent peacefulness. Archaeologists have found no signs of an army, no battle wounds on recovered bones, no partially destroyed buildings, and few weapons. So what happened to the Harappans? Experts think that the Indus River may have changed its path, leading to failed crops and catastrophic flooding. The Harappan people dwindled, and their culture vanished.

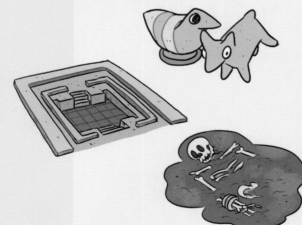

The streets were laid out in a grid.

People had good personal hygiene.

The society was peaceful, as buried bodies do not show signs of violence.

They had a system of writing.

Kids played games.

BONUS: Egyptologists think that 30,000 people, working in teams, built the Great Pyramid. Some teams inscribed their names, such as "Friends of Khufu," inside the pyramid, leading experts to believe that the teams competed and felt a sense of pride in their work. Based on your own experience, does this inference make sense? Explain your answer.

_____
_____
_____
_____

Now add this
sticker to your map!

Around the Clock

Fill in each blank with a word from the box that pairs with each bolded correlative conjunction.

| ~~either~~ | ~~but~~ | ~~and~~ | ~~whether~~ | ~~not only~~ | ~~neither~~ |

Conjunctions

The name Big Ben refers to **both** the bell inside Elizabeth Tower
__*and*__ the tower itself.

Big Ben was named for __*either*__ Sir Benjamin Hall, the first commissioner of works, **or** heavyweight boxing champion Benjamin Caunt.

Elizabeth Tower is **not** open to overseas tourists, __*but*__ U.K. residents can request a visit in writing.

The lighting of the clock faces depends on __*neither*__ **or not** Parliament is in session.

__*not only*__ did the first Big Ben crack irreparably, **but** the second Big Ben—the present one—is also slightly cracked.

During the upcoming refurbishment of Elizabeth Tower, the clock will __*whether*__ chime **nor** strike.

Brain Box

Correlative conjunctions are words that pair up in a sentence to link words or phrases. Some common correlative conjunctions are: both . . . and, either . . . or, whether . . . or, neither . . . nor, not only . . . but also, not . . . but, not so much . . . as.

Watch Your Step!

Place parentheses around two numbers in each expression to make the expression true.

Using Parentheses

$50 - 5 \times (2 + 1) = \mathbf{35}$

$(50 - 5) \times 2 + 1 = 45 \times 2 + 1 = 90 + 1 = 91$ Incorrect
$50 - (5 \times 2) + 1 = 50 - 10 + 1 = 41$ Incorrect
$50 - 5 \times (2 + 1) = 50 - 5 \times 3 = 50 - 15 = 35$ Correct!

$(50 - 5) \times 2 + 1 = \mathbf{91}$

$(12 \times 3) - 2 + 1 = \mathbf{33}$

$12 \times (3 - 2) + 1 = \mathbf{13}$

$6 \div 3 \times (2 + 4) = \mathbf{12}$

$6 \div (3 \times 2) + 4 = \mathbf{5}$

Upon completion, add these stickers to your path on the map!

Brain Box

Follow the **order of operations:**

Complete operations within parentheses first.

Then find the value of exponents.

Then multiply and divide from left to right.

Then add and subtract from left to right.

Write a numerical expression using parentheses if necessary. Then solve.

A family of 6 went on a donkey ride down into the Grand Canyon. The cost was $294 per person. They had a coupon for $55 off the total cost. What was the final cost?

294
x   6
1,764

1,764
- 55
1,709

$1709

.1054
+.945
1999 × 2

A limousine tour of the Grand Canyon costs $498 per person. A bus tour to the canyon costs $149 per person. How much more is one limousine tour than two bus tours?

498
- 149
349

$349

Brain Box

The helicopter descended twice as far as the sum of 945 feet and 1,054 feet. How far down into the canyon did the helicopter fly?

2 × (945 + 1054)

2998 feet

If you need parentheses ( ) and brackets [ ] in the same expression, put the parentheses inside the brackets. Then calculate from the inside out.

A day trip from Las Vegas to the Grand Canyon is 10 hours and 30 minutes long and includes stops at other attractions. If you spend 3 hours and 30 minutes at the Grand Canyon, how many minutes are spent on travel and other attractions?

7 hrs.

A local round-trip tour involves a 45-minute drive each way to and from the Grand Canyon and 2 hours at the viewpoint. How many minutes longer is that than a tour that takes a total of 3 hours?

15 mins

BONUS: You and 4 friends go on a helicopter ride over the Grand Canyon. The cost is $189 per person. You have a coupon for a $50 discount on the total cost. How much will each person pay if you divide the final cost equally? Write the expression using parentheses and brackets. Then solve.

Now add this sticker to your map!

Motion and Stability

I Like to Move It, Move It

Read the passage. Then write whether each picture is an example of Newton's first, second, or third law of motion.

Motion is the process by which an object changes its position. Sir Isaac Newton wrote three **laws of motion**.

1 An object in motion stays in motion, unless an external force acts upon it. For example: An ice skater glides across the ice until the friction of the ice causes her to slow down.

2 Force equals mass times acceleration. For example: The heavier a box, the more force needed to push it forward. To accelerate the speed of the moving box, even more force is needed.

3 For every action, there is an equal and opposite reaction. For example: The action of a basketball hitting the floor causes it to bounce back up.

Upon completion, add this sticker to your path on the map!

A swimmer kicks and water splashes.

A feather sails and falls to the ground because of air friction and gravity.

It takes two people to push a stalled car two miles per hour.

An ant carries a seed many times its body weight three inches per second.

A tumbleweed rolls until it hits a cactus.

BONUS: Complete the sentence: As a cobra's mass increases, it will need to use more _____ to strike at its prey.

Now add this sticker to your map!

Hail, Augustus

Read the passage. Study the map of the Roman Empire under Augustus. Circle Rome (*Roma*) and Athens (*Athenae*). Then answer the questions.

Rome grew from a city, founded along the Tiber River in 753 BCE, to an empire that spanned much of Europe, the Middle East, and North Africa. During its years as a republic (a nation or territory with elected officials), Rome began conquering other lands under the military leadership of Julius Caesar. His nephew Augustus rose to power in 27 BCE, becoming the first emperor of Rome. The empire grew, but eventually Rome could no longer hold itself together as a unified empire or ward off foreign military powers. In 476 CE, Rome fell.

What body of water lies in the center of the Roman Empire?

_____

Was Athens part of the Roman Empire under Augustus?

_____

Before trains, planes, and motorized vehicles, why would it be advantageous to have a sea at the center of the Roman Empire?

_____

_____

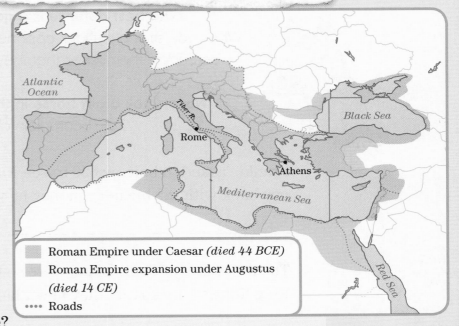

Roman Empire under Caesar (*died 44 BCE*)
Roman Empire expansion under Augustus (*died 14 CE*)
•••• Roads

The Romans were tolerant of multiple religions and often adopted the religious beliefs of the people they conquered. Knowing this, why might Greek and Roman gods be so similar to each other?

_____

_____

_____

Upon completion, add this sticker to your path on the map!

Good Advice

Read each proverb and its meaning. Then choose the proverb that offers the best advice for each situation.

The time to repair the roof is when the sun is shining.
It's best to do something before there is an urgent need.

Don't count your chickens before they hatch.
Don't make plans based on a good outcome
about which you can't be sure.

Don't put all your eggs in one basket.
Don't invest all your time and resources into any one plan.

The best defense is a good offense.
When you strongly attack opponents, your opponents are so busy
defending themselves that they can't launch their own attack.

Never look a gift horse in the mouth.
Don't complain about gifts.

Frankie asked to borrow $20 to see *King Kong*, which he said he would pay back with the birthday money he would probably get.

_____

The dinosaurs of Skull Island were so busy defending their territory from King Kong's attacks that they never launched an attack of their own.

_____

Jake's grandmother gave him a remote-control helicopter for his birthday, but what he had really wanted was cash.

_____

Lydia didn't understand why her mother made her save for the trip to London that was several months away.

_____

Carl didn't worry about his other movie projects; *King Kong* would make him rich and famous.

_____

Upon
completion,
add this
sticker to
your path on
the map!

Brain Box

A **proverb** is an expression of wisdom that has significance beyond its literal meaning.

Variety Is the Spice of Life

Write a five-sentence paragraph about a food that is special to you. Then complete the chart to determine whether your sentences are varied.

Varied Sentences

_____

_____

_____

_____

_____

_____

_____

Sentence	Number of Words	Simple, Compound, or Complex?
First		
Second		
Third		
Fourth		
Fifth		

Upon completion, add this sticker to your path on the map!

Subtract the number of words in the shortest sentence from the number of words in the longest sentence._____

Count the number of sentence types you have. (If you have one or more simple sentences, add 1. For one or more compound sentences, add 1. If you have one or more complex sentences, add 1.)_____

Use the key below to judge whether or not your writing is spicy. Circle the category that fits your writing.

15 and above: Hot, hot, hot! You varied your sentences for a spicy blend!

10–15: Mild-hot. Your sentences are somewhat varied. You are on the right track.

Under 10: Pass the pepper sauce, please. Try varying your sentences to make your writing more flavorful!

This Is Sparta!
And Athens!

Read about Sparta and Athens.

Sparta and Athens were city-states in Ancient Greece. Though both were powerful and had systems of government that considered the will of the people, they were very different from each other.

The Spartan government had two kings. They led a council of 28 elder citizens, which in turn consulted a council of all free Spartan men age 30 and over. This form of government is called an oligarchy.

Spartans relied on food grown in its territories by large numbers of slaves called Helots. Because the Helots greatly outnumbered the Spartans, Sparta feared they might rebel, and built up its military to prepare for potential uprisings.

In fact, Sparta's primary focus was to maintain a strong military. Boys trained for military service beginning at age 7, and from ages 20 to 30 they lived in military barracks away from their families. In battle, their aim was to win or die. Women and girls had more rights and opportunities than in other Greek city-states. Girls learned to read and write, and participated in sports such as running and wrestling. Women could own property, and many owned land.

In contrast, life in Athens revolved around building a democracy. To this end, citizens were educated so that they could make sound decisions for the state. However, only free males were considered citizens. (Slavery persisted in Athens, too, but not to the extent of Sparta.) Athenian boys were educated in reading, writing, math, and music. At age 20, they attained the right to vote, own property, debate issues, and more—they could hear court cases, appoint army generals, and be appointed to a council that proposed laws and negotiated with foreign powers. Women and girls had no such rights or opportunities.

Though life in Athens wasn't centered around its military, the Athenian army was strong. When Athens clashed with Persia over territory in Asia, the Athenian army was victorious. Athens later joined forces with Sparta to defeat Persia again. Infighting among the city-states eventually weakened the Greek Empire, and it was conquered.

Brain Box

Dating to 3000 BCE, **Greek civilization** gave rise to democracy, philosophy, and the Olympics. Around 750 BCE, city-states developed. The most powerful, Sparta and Athens, were by turns allies and rivals. For hundreds of years, Greece managed to ward off invaders, but it was eventually conquered by Macedonia, and later the Roman Empire. Greek culture survived, however, and was often adopted by its invaders.

Fill out the chart with true or false.

	Athens	Sparta
Women can own property.		
The military is strong.		
Education of both sexes is paramount.		
Slavery is legal.		
Men live in military barracks for 10 years.		

Classical Greece

Write a paragraph stating whether you would rather live in Sparta or Athens and why.

_____

_____

_____

_____

_____

_____

_____

_____

Upon completion, add these stickers to your path on the map!

BONUS: The Fontaines de la Concorde in Paris commemorate commerce and industry in France. Imagine you are an ancient fountain designer. Draw a fountain that reflects either Athenian or Spartan values.

Now add this sticker to your map!

Analyze
Pattern
Relationships

Lean on Math

The Leaning Tower of Pisa leans at about a 4-degree angle.
Complete the patterns and chart to see how far a tower
might lean if it followed these rules.

4°

Doubtful Designer's tower leans 1 degree more each year.
The pattern rule is add 1.

Poor Planner's tower leans 2 degrees more each year.
The pattern rule is add 2.

Bad Builder's tower leans 6 degrees more each year.
The pattern rule is add 6.

Year	0	1	2	3	4	5
Doubtful Designer's Tower	0°	1°	2°	3°	4°	5°
Poor Planner's Tower	0°	2°	4°	6°	8°	10°
Bad Builder's Tower	0°	6°	12°	18°	24°	30°

Compare corresponding terms of two patterns at a time.

Each year Poor Planner's tower leans ___2X___ as many degrees
as Doubtful Designer's tower.
Write the pattern for that rule. _P-P goes by two7_

Each year Bad Builder's tower leans ___6X___ as many degrees
as Doubtful Designer's tower.
Write the pattern for that rule. _1x6=6 6X1=6_

Each year Bad Builder's tower leans ___3X___ as many degrees
as Poor Planner's tower.
Write the pattern for that rule. _7√6=3 3x2ee_

Upon
completion,
add this
sticker to
your path on
the map!

Brain Box

Each number in a pattern is called a **term. Corresponding terms** are those
that appear in the same position (1st, 2nd, 3rd, etc.) in the two patterns.

Pattern A	0	1	2	3	4	5
Pattern B	0	4	8	12	16	20

1 and 4 are corresponding terms; 2 and 8 are corresponding terms; Pattern B is
4 times Pattern A. The pattern for that rule is 4, 8, 12, 16 . . . and so on.

Level 2 complete!

Add this achievement sticker
to your path...

...and move on to

Level 3!

Evolution

Brain Box

Evolution is the process by which organisms develop **traits** over time that help them to survive in their environment.

Meet the Marsupials

Read about koalas and Tasmanian devils. Then fill in the Venn diagram using the traits from the box.

Tasmanian devil

- A rear-facing pouch, in which multiple immature cubs feed on milk

- Sharp claws for tearing meat

- Strong jaws and sharp teeth for eating all animal parts, including bones and fur

- Juvenile wrestling behavior to prepare the cubs for the competition they will face as adults when feeding on carcasses

Koala

- A pouch, in which a single immature cub feeds on milk

- Sharp claws for climbing

- Sharp front teeth and strong molars specialized for cutting and chewing leaves

- 18 to 22 hours per day of sleep, which allows the koala to conserve the little energy it derives from its low-calorie diet of eucalyptus leaves

Traits

sharp teeth   multiple cubs   sharp claws   single cub   produce milk

competitive behavior   ample sleep   carnivore   herbivore

koala   **Tasmanian devil**

both

Australia

Study the physical map of Australia and answer the questions.

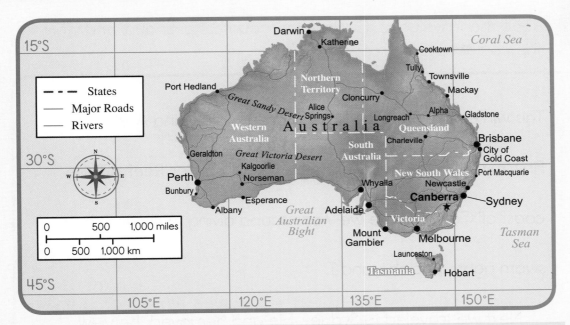

In what state is Sydney located?

_____

Which state is also an island?

_____

Is the Coral Sea located along Australia's east or west coast?

_____

The two largest Australian deserts are named on this map.
Are they located in Eastern or Western Australia?

_____

Based on context clues on the map, what is a bight?

| an inland sea | an open bay | a bog |

Upon completion, add this sticker to your path on the map!

BONUS: Tasmania is located below 40 degrees latitude, whereas the Northern Territory nearly reaches 10 degrees latitude. Underline which hypothesis you could make about the weather in the two regions based on their positions in relation to the equator.

It is warmer on average in the Northern Territory than in Tasmania.

The Northern Territory has cold winters, but Tasmania does not.

Now add this sticker to your map!

A Case of Mistaken Cases

Read the travelogue. Circle each incorrect pronoun, and write the correct pronoun above it.

Pronouns

This winter, I fulfilled me lifelong dream of visiting Australia.

First, my mom and me visited the Great Barrier Reef off the coast of Cairns. While we were scuba diving, a clown fish swam right up to she and I.

Next we traveled to Sydney. Me and her loved the view of the Opera House. The tour wouldn't have been complete without a trip to the outback. Traveling by bus across the desert, we saw kangaroos, emus, and crocodiles. We were warned not to take selfies with the crocodiles, as them are known to attack. Yikes! Finally, us traveled to the western city of Perth. There, me and my mom surfed some of the biggest waves we'd ever seen.

I absolutely loved Australia!

Brain Box

If a pronoun replaces the subject of a sentence, it should be in the **subjective case** (I, we, he, she, it, they). If a pronoun replaces the object of a sentence, it should be in the **objective case** (me, us, him, her, it, them). When a pronoun describes possession, it should be in the **possessive case** (my, our, his, her, its, their).

Every Single One

Rewrite each sentence so that the noun and pronoun are both either singular or plural. (HINT: You may need to change the verb as well.)

As a reader grows more confident, they choose more challenging books.

_____

A babysitter must be able to multitask, or else they will quickly become overwhelmed.

_____

A basketball player usually perfects their shooting outside of team practice.

_____

If someone from camp calls, tell them I just stepped out for a minute.

_____

_____

BONUS: Write a sentence about a koala that includes a singular pronoun. Then write a sentence about a group of koalas that includes a plural pronoun.

_____

_____

_____

Now add this sticker to your map!

Brain Box

If a pronoun refers to one person, it should be **singular.** If the pronoun refers to more than one person, it should be **plural.**

Examples: If **a player** scores, **he or she** advances. If **players** score, **they** advance.

Hopping Good!

Find each product.

$$\begin{array}{r} 359 \\ \times\ 4 \\ \hline \end{array}$$

$$\begin{array}{r} 74 \\ \times\ 16 \\ \hline \end{array}$$

$$\begin{array}{r} 429 \\ \times\ 51 \\ \hline \end{array}$$

$$\begin{array}{r} 726 \\ \times\ 3 \\ \hline \end{array}$$

$$\begin{array}{r} 39 \\ \times\ 48 \\ \hline \end{array}$$

$$\begin{array}{r} 371 \\ \times\ 88 \\ \hline \end{array}$$

Brain Box

You can use **partial products** to multiply. Multiply each digit in the bottom factor by the numbers in the ones, tens, and hundreds places. Then add the partial products.

```
 127
 x 2
   14 ← 2 x 7
   40 ← 2 x 20
+200 ← 2 x 100
  254
```

```
  28
 x 15
   40 ← 5 x 8
  100 ← 5 x 20
   80 ← 10 x 8
+ 200 ← 10 x 20
  420
```

```
   353
  x 47
    21 ← 7 x 3
   350 ← 7 x 50
  2100 ← 7 x 300
   120 ← 40 x 3
  2000 ← 40 x 50
+12000 ← 40 x 300
16,591
```

You can also use partial products with the **box method**. Break apart factors by place value and multiply. Then reassemble the numbers by adding them back together to find the final product.

```
 127
 x 2
```

2	100 +	20 +	7
	200	40	14

```
 200
  40
+ 14
 254
```

Multiplication
Strategies

815
× 9

536
× 72

473
× 56

295
× 46

317
× 81

64
× 92

864
× 13

Upon
completion,
add these
stickers to
your path on
the map!

Brain Box

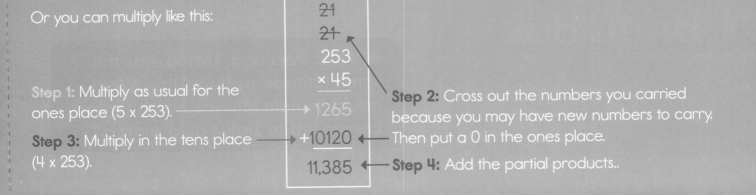

Or you can multiply like this:

~~21~~
~~21~~
253
× 45
1265
+10120
11,385

Step 1: Multiply as usual for the ones place (5 × 253).

Step 2: Cross out the numbers you carried because you may have new numbers to carry. Then put a 0 in the ones place.

Step 3: Multiply in the tens place (4 × 253).

Step 4: Add the partial products.

Climate

What in the World?

Study the map. Then draw a line to connect each location with the explanation of the landscape.

In polar regions, landmasses with high elevations are covered in ice year round, whereas landmasses with lower elevations tend to have a tundra biome, meaning that surface snow and ice melts during part of the year.

Greenland

Eastern Canada

Amazon Rain Forest

Along the equator, winds from the Northern Hemisphere and Southern Hemisphere converge, carrying precipitation. As a result, the world's largest rain forests are found along the equator.

Brain Box

Climate is the weather in a certain place, usually over a 30-year period. Climate can change over time. Currently, dry regions are getting dryer, wet regions, wetter, and most regions, warmer.

BONUS: Portland, Maine, has the same latitude as Pisa, Italy. What could explain Maine's harsh winters compared to Italy's mild winters?

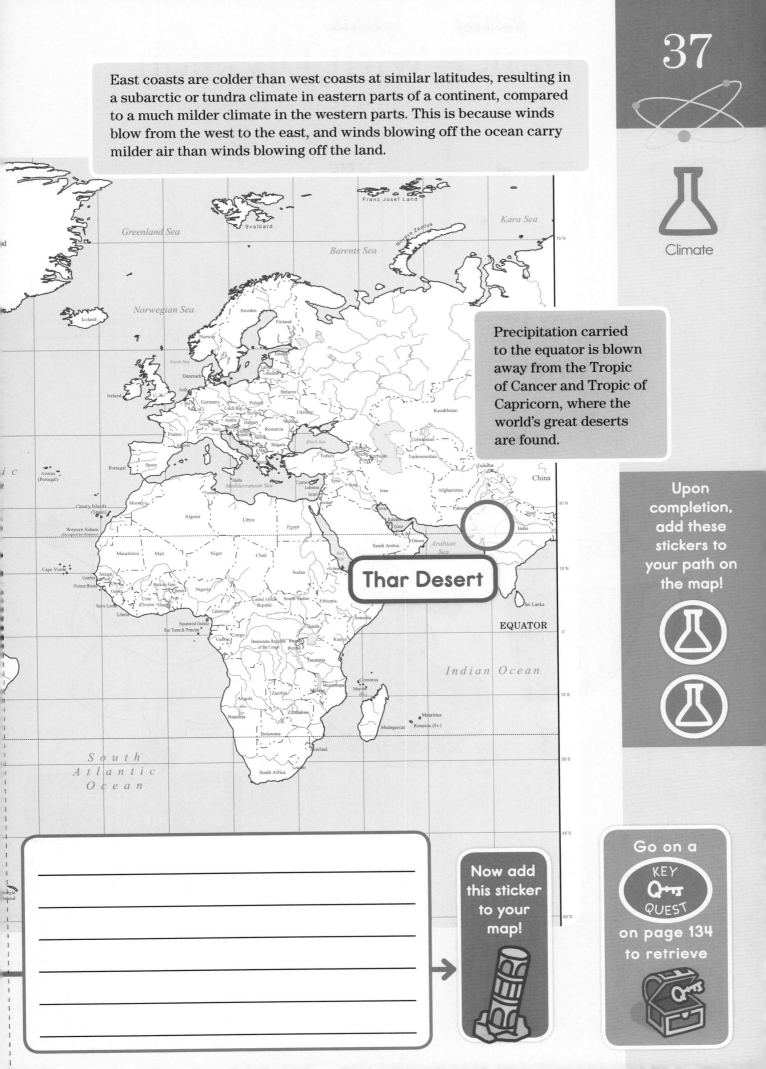

East coasts are colder than west coasts at similar latitudes, resulting in a subarctic or tundra climate in eastern parts of a continent, compared to a much milder climate in the western parts. This is because winds blow from the west to the east, and winds blowing off the ocean carry milder air than winds blowing off the land.

Precipitation carried to the equator is blown away from the Tropic of Cancer and Tropic of Capricorn, where the world's great deserts are found.

Thar Desert

EQUATOR

Upon completion, add these stickers to your path on the map!

Now add this sticker to your map!

Go on a KEY QUEST on page 134 to retrieve

Division
Strategies

Dance with Division

Divide by a one-digit number. Find each quotient and remainder, if any.

3)343

9)675

4)924

6)5,298

3)3,702

5)3,239

Brain Box

One way to divide a large number by a one-digit number is like this:

Step 1: Divide into the hundreds.

Step 2: Multiply and subtract.

Step 3: Bring down the tens.
Then divide into the tens.

Step 4: Multiply and subtract again.

Step 5: Bring down the ones and divide into the ones.

Step 6: Multiply and subtract. If there is a remainder, write it next to the quotient.

quotient → 136 r2
divisor → 7)954 ← dividend
-7↓
25
-21↓
44
-42
2 ← remainder

BONUS: A specialty store has 1,040 costumes divided equally into outfits for 20 different types of traditional dances. If a square-dance team wanted to buy matching costumes, how many could they buy?

Divide by a two-digit number. Find each quotient and remainder, if any.

23)5,129

18)6,948

32)7,264

83)2,241

61)2,135

87)3,828

Division Strategies

Upon completion, add these stickers to your path on the map!

Now add this sticker to your map!

Brain Box

You can divide a large number by a two-digit number like this:

Step 1: Divide into the hundreds. If that is not possible, divide into the tens.

Step 2: Multiply and subtract.

Step 3: Bring down the ones. Then divide into the ones.

Step 4: Multiply and subtract again. If there is a remainder, write it next to the quotient.

$$\begin{array}{r} 47 \\ 23\overline{)1081} \\ -92\downarrow \\ \hline 161 \\ -161 \\ \hline 0 \end{array}$$

Division

Quokka Quotients

Find each quotient. Then draw a line to the correct equation to check your answer.

$19\overline{)722}$

$36\overline{)2,270}$

$48\overline{)2,160}$

$92\overline{)4,692}$

$67\overline{)1,685}$

Upon completion, add this sticker to your path on the map!

Brain Box

You can check the answer to a division problem by multiplying the quotient and the divisor. Then add the remainder, if there is one. The answer should be the same as the dividend.

$36 \times 63 + 2 =$

$38 \times 19 =$

$45 \times 48 =$

$92 \times 51 =$

$25 \times 67 + 10 =$

Adorable Animals

Read the passage and underline the words that have incorrect **able** and **ible** endings. Then spell them correctly below.

Spelling

What looks like a rat, is as big as a cat, and is totally lovible? It's the quokka, a marsupial living in Australia. On the mainland, invasive species such as foxes have hunted the quokka to lower numbers, but they're still prevalent on surrounding islands. Because the animals are furry and cute

(they have the appearance of always smiling), visitors have taken a shine to the quokka. In turn, the quokkas have become quite comfortible around people, and will even pose in selfies with them! #Adorible! Experts say that while taking a picture is harmless, other behaviors are undesirible. Visitors should refrain from touching the animals (however huggible they appear). And feeding a quokka is an especially terrable idea. The adaptible quokka will readily eat people food, but it gets stuck in its teeth, making the quokka vulnerible to infection. So remember, it's okay to say *cheese* with a quokka. Just don't feed it cheese afterwards.

Upon completion, add this sticker to your path on the map!

_____ _____

_____ _____

_____

_____

Brain Box

The suffix **able** is more common than the suffix **ible.** The roots of words ending in able are usually complete words. Example: adapt**able**. The roots of words ending in ible are often not complete words. Example: horr**ible**.

Pyramid Scheme

Study the diagram and read about feudalism. Then write down three societal problems that may have arisen because of this system.

Feudal Societies

Upon completion, add this sticker to your path on the map!

With the fall of Rome in 476 CE, the Middle Ages began. During this time, feudalism emerged in Western Europe.

In the feudal system, the king granted land to powerful nobles in exchange for loyalty and service to the king.

Each powerful noble granted land to knights in exchange for loyalty and military service. Thus, each knight pledged military service to a specific noble—and not to the king or the country.

The knights and nobles "granted" serfs small plots of land to farm in exchange for their labor. In fact, the serfs weren't allowed to leave that land without the lord's permission. The serfs owed the lord a portion of the produce from their own fields and also had to work in the lord's fields. In addition, the serfs were required to use the lord's equipment, like the mill for grinding grain, for instance, all for a high price.

_____

_____

_____

BONUS: How did the fractured system of government (with knights fighting for individual nobles as opposed to one united kingdom) make feudal Europe and Britain vulnerable to attacks from raiders like the Vikings?

_____

_____

_____

_____

Now add this sticker to your map!

Level 3 complete!

Add this achievement sticker to your path...

...and move on to

Level 4A

on page 44!

...or
move on to

Level 4B

on page 56!

Beetle-Mania

Travel the world, and you'll find beetles everywhere! Write a math sentence to compare the length of beetles using >, =, or <.

Comparing Decimals to Thousandths

START LEVEL 4A HERE!

Southern U.S. 0.4 inches

Germany 0.236 inches

India 0.461 inches

Italy 0.118 inches

Kenya 1.142 inches

North Africa 0.492 inches

Mexico 5.118 inches

Thailand 1.26 inches

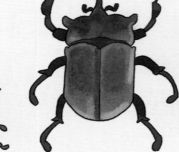
Turkey 0.551 inches

Peru 0.504 inches

Mexico ◯ Germany

Mexico ◯ South America

Austria ◯ Sweden

Sweden ◯ Italy

Southern U.S. ◯ India

Brain Box

Compare digits in the same place value position. If they are the same, move to the next place value position to the right and compare.

Remember, you can write zeros at the end of a decimal without changing the value.

2.5 = 2.50 = 2.500

    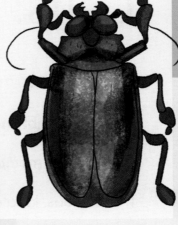

Eastern U.S.
2.4 inches

Sweden
0.123 inches

Southeast Asia
2.25 inches

Austria
0.157 inches

South America
6.7 inches

Peru ◯ Turkey

North Africa ◯ Italy

Peru ◯ North Africa

Thailand ◯ Kenya

Eastern U.S. ◯ Southeast Asia

Answer each question according to the information given above.

You find a beetle in your yard that is 0.5 inches long. How does that compare with the beetle from Peru? Write a math sentence to support your answer.

_____

You find a beetle that is $2\frac{1}{2}$ inches long. Which of the beetles shown is closest to that measurement?

_____

A 10-year-old's hand is about 6.5 inches wide. Which beetle is longer than that?

_____

Upon completion, add these stickers to your path on the map!

Cells

Cells: Small But Mighty

Read about the parts of the animal cell. Then follow the directions to color the parts of the cell.

The **cell membrane** is the outer case of the cell.

The **nuclear membrane** is the outer case of the nucleus.

The **nucleus**, located at the center of the cell, controls the cell's activity.

Each cell nucleus contains an organism's entire DNA sequence. **Chromatin** describes both the structure that contains the DNA, the DNA itself, and the RNA, which helps the cell express its DNA.

Mitochondria, located outside the nucleus, absorbs nutrients and transforms them into energy needed by the cell to complete its functions.

Cytoplasm is the liquid inside a cell that protects the cell's parts so that they do not collide.

Upon completion, add this sticker to your path on the map!

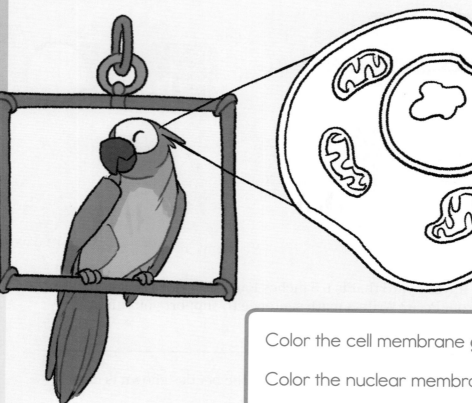

Color the cell membrane **green**.

Color the nuclear membrane **orange**.

Color the nucleus **pink**.

Color the chromatin **blue**.

Color the mitochondria **purple**.

Color the cytoplasm **yellow**.

Brain Box

A **cell** is the smallest possible living unit. An organism can be made up of one or more cells. In a multicellular organism, such as a parrot, certain types of cells form tissues, which make up organs, including the brain.

Land of Plenty

Read the introductory paragraph and list of facts. Circle the facts that support the main idea of the introductory paragraph.

Native Americans of the Pacific Northwest, such as the Haida, Coast Salish, and Ilingit peoples, were hunters and gatherers. However, these societies more closely mirrored the social hierarchies of agricultural societies. Historically, agricultural societies have been socially stratified due to the surplus of food available. That is, some members of society benefit from the surplus more than others, making them wealthier and sometimes more revered. In contrast, hunter-gatherer societies have tended to be egalitarian. However, food was so plentiful in the Pacific Northwest that the surplus food resulted in different social classes.

Parents tried to arrange marriages with young men and women of equal or higher status.

If young people from the lower or middle class proved themselves to be talented or remarkable in some way, they could "marry up" in status.

Upper-class children were formally trained in etiquette.

Summer was the busiest time for Pacific Northwest people, as they fished, gathered, and preserved food for winter.

People traveled in small groups to various home sites in the summer but reunited in their villages in the winter.

During winter, high-class people often focused on social obligations and art, having slaves do their day-to-day labor.

Art from the Pacific Northwest, as seen on sculptures such as totem poles, was bold and stylized.

Pacific Northwest people used the plentiful wood available to build huge homes, buildings, and dugout canoes.

Upon completion, add this sticker to your path on the map!

Mutations

Read the examples of human mutations. Circle whether they are helpful, harmful, both helpful and harmful, or neither helpful nor harmful.

Heredity

Lactase Digestion

Around 7,500 years ago, a genetic mutation gave some people the ability to produce lactase, which allowed them to drink animal milk without getting sick. People who raised cows could now drink their milk for needed nutrition.

helpful	harmful	both helpful and harmful	neither helpful nor harmful

Upon completion, add this sticker to your path on the map!

Blue Eyes

All humans used to have brown eyes. Then roughly 6,000 to 10,000 years ago, a genetic mutation disrupted the production of melanin, which causes eyes to be brown. The color was diluted to blue. This created the first ever blue-eyed person.

helpful	harmful	both helpful and harmful	neither helpful nor harmful

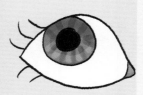

Sickle Cell Mutation

When the sickle cell mutation is inherited from both parents, it causes the painful disease sickle cell anemia. However, the same mutation protects people from malaria, a disease spread by mosquitoes. So a person who inherits just one sickle cell gene can actually have a healthier life than a person without the gene.

helpful	harmful	both helpful and harmful	neither helpful nor harmful

Brain Box

Genes are segments of DNA that code for building proteins. Proteins, in turn, form the structures and functions of each individual and affect traits such as eyesight. Humans have two variants of most genes—one from each parent. Sometimes only one variant affects a trait; in other cases, both variants work together to produce the trait. Sometimes the original gene develops a mutation so that it is different from either parent's gene and may change a trait.

Alike, But Different

Read the two definitions and the scrambled word. Then write the unscrambled word, which fits both definitions.

Homographs

sporting apparatus used to hit a ball OR a flying mammal

tba

to endure (a difficult situation) OR a large omnivorous mammal

reba

**to stop a car and leave it in place OR
a public area used for leisure and recreation**

prak

a cliff OR to mislead

flbfu

**to not notice something important OR
a place from which a view can be seen below**

lorevoko

**to move back and forth or side to side OR
a solid substance formed by pressure or heat**

cork

the movement of air OR to move in a twisting and turning way

diwn

**a telling of real or imagined events
OR a level of a building**

rosyt

Upon completion, add this sticker to your path on the map!

Brain Box

Homographs are words that are spelled alike but differ in meaning and sometimes pronunciation.

YOU'VE REACHED LEVEL 4A'S GATEWAY.

If you have unlock the gate by adding to your map. If not, retrace your steps to find the key!

Line 'Em Up

Add the decimals. Regroup where necessary.

Add
Decimals

```
  46.5
+ 36.29
  82.79
```

```
  3.72
+ 4.13
  7.85
```

```
  18.266
+  9.57
  27.836
```

```
   0.123
+ 54.9
    ?
```

```
   91.9
+ 123.228
  215.128
```

```
  217.04
+  55.106
  272.146
```

$63.098 + 11.9 = \underline{63.217}$

```
63.098
  11.9
63.215
```

$1.55 + 12.3 + 11.406 = \underline{25.256}$

```
 1.55
12.3
11.406
25256
```

$7.4 + 4.77 = \underline{5.51}$

```
 4.77
 7.4
5.51
```

Subtract the decimals.
Regroup where necessary.

$$2\ 12$$
$$0.321$$
$$-\ 0.16$$
$$0.305$$

$$8.6$$
$$-\ 4.2$$
$$4.4$$

$$45.7$$
$$-\ 10.49$$
$$56.19$$

$$73.44$$
$$-\ 31.18$$
$$42.26$$

$$99.7524$$
$$-\ 0.852$$
$$66.72$$

Subtract
Decimals

**Upon
completion,
add these
stickers to
your path on
the map!**

$$55.43 - 4.33 = \underline{51.10}$$

$$9.2$$
$$-\ 1.52$$
$$7.72$$

$$71.05 - 1.6 = \underline{69.9}$$

2

69.9

Brain Box

To add or subtract decimals, line up the decimal
points and write 0 as a placeholder if necessary.
Then add or subtract as if with whole numbers. Align
the decimal point in the answer too.

$$6.285 - 2.08 = \underline{6.077}$$

$$100.47$$
$$+\ 2.40$$
$$102.87$$

$$367.50$$
$$-\ 1.36$$
$$366.14$$

Emmeline

Read the poem by William Wordsworth and the biographical note.
Then answer the questions.

Poetry

3

To a Butterfly

STAY near me—do not take thy flight!
A little longer stay in sight!
Much converse do I find in thee,
Historian of my infancy!
Float near me; do not yet depart!
Dead times revive in thee:
Thou bring'st, gay creature as thou art!
A solemn image to my heart,
My father's family!

Oh! pleasant, pleasant were the days,
The time, when, in our childish plays,
My sister Emmeline and I
Together chased the butterfly!
A very hunter did I rush
Upon the prey: with leaps and spring
I followed on from brake to bush;
But she, God love her, feared to brush
The dust from off its wings.

William Wordsworth wrote this poem about his sister Dorothy
(Emmeline in the poem), from whom he was separated at age 8
when their mother died and Dorothy was sent to live with a cousin.
Dorothy and William didn't see each other again until adulthood,
when they became close companions.

Based on the title, to whom do you think the narrator is speaking?

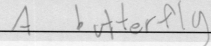
A butterfly

Poetry

Based on the content of the second stanza, what might the lines from the first stanza, "Much converse do I find in thee/Historian of my infancy," mean? Circle one.

You remind me of my childhood.

You are talkative.

You are a professor of history.

How would you describe the brother and sister's relationship? Circle one.

They were rivals.

They were friends.

They weren't very close.

The "dust" on butterfly wings could be interpreted as scales, and losing too many scales can be harmful to a butterfly. Knowing this, what does it tell you about Emmeline that she feared to brush the "dust" from the butterfly's wings?

She didn't grow up.

In contrast, how did the narrator chase the butterfly?

by running

Upon completion, add these stickers to your path on the map!

What is the tone of the poem? Circle one.

Angry

Elated

Bittersweet

4

Based on the poem and biographical note, what can you infer is the theme of the poem? Circle one.

Everybody has to grow up sometime.

The loveliest memories are the most fragile.

Humans destroy nature through their greed.

Mayan Innovations

Read about Mayan inventions and innovations. Then find the bold words in the word search.

The Mayans lived in present-day Mexico, Belize, Guatemala, El Salvador, and Honduras. Through technology and innovation, they transformed their harsh environment into a civilization that supported about as many people per square mile as Los Angeles does today. They did this through a system of farming that included landfilling, **fertilization**, and **irrigation**. In addition to food crops, Mayans cultivated the **rubber** plant, which they used to make balls, glue, and waterproof cloth.

The Mayans had among them brilliant mathematicians. By observing the stars, they devised an accurate 365-day **calendar**. This helped farmers know when to plant and harvest. Meanwhile, engineers designed **pyramids** and **palaces**. Incredibly, these were built without the use of a wheel and axle, which hadn't been invented in the region. Mayan civilization lasted 2,000 years and reached its height between roughly 300 CE to 900 CE.

When the Spanish **conquistadors** arrived, they burned Mayan books and outlawed the system of writing. Though Mayans still live in the region today, they are long separated from the ancient written language. Scholars now **decipher** the books and carvings that remain and are learning the true history of the Mayans.

N L L K U H P R E F F E O I O
U O D B M Z E P W S E P S X M
I J I H J H Z A P Y R A M I D
D F C T P K B L B W T K Q Z P
Z N L I A D W A Q H I G T J Y
A O C C V G M C C Y L B O R W
R E L F P V I E Q S I Z I R L
D U T F M S E R S B Z V E P R
Q Q B M V Z B J R D A F Y G A
I T I B A E P U E I T I N A D
Q U B U E D A K B X I G K J N
K X G L J R M D F H O N B T E
S R O D A T S I U Q N O C V L
S G W R T L P U U R F L P D A
G B V P Z X K P Z F O G E N C

Level 4A complete!

Add this achievement sticker to your path...

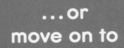

...and move on to

Level 5C

on page 86!

...or
move on to

Level 5A

on page 74!

Nomadic Language

Read the meaning of each **Greek** or **Latin** prefix and suffix. Then fill in the blanks with the correct affixes.

Latin and
Greek Affixes
and Roots

START
LEVEL
4B
HERE!

ab- Latin: away from	**camp-** Latin: field
acm- Greek: point	**hibern-** Latin: wintry
acr- Greek: extreme height, summit	**contra-** Latin: against
am- Latin: love, like, friend	**mater-** Latin: mother
anthropo- Greek: human	**-scribe** Latin: to write
botan- Greek: plant	**-phobia** Greek: fear

Poor Chloe was _____sent, so she missed our field trip to Athens.

As the tour bus revved its engine, Marcus jumped; he had phono_____, which is the fear of loud noises.

We visited the _____opolis first, so named because it sits high above the city.

Our tour guide was an _____iable person and seemed to be friends with everybody at the Acropolis Museum.

The carving of Athena adjusting her sandal shows how the gods were _____morphized—given human characteristics.

Knowledgeable in _____y, Aria knew that the olive tree atop the Acropolis couldn't be the same one referenced in the story of Athena and the olive tree.

At the graveyard, Persephone touched the stone, which was in_____d with the names of soldiers who had died in an ancient war.

At the end of the day, we relaxed at our _____site—a beautiful field overlooking the Mediterranean.

Latin and Greek Affixes and Roots

Upon completion, add these stickers to your path on the map!

BONUS: Write a sentence about a travel experience that includes one of the Greek or Latin roots or affixes from the list.

_____
_____
_____

Now add this sticker to your map!

Dictionary
and
Thesaurus

Forest, Jungle, Wood

Read the thesaurus and dictionary selections below.

THESAURUS

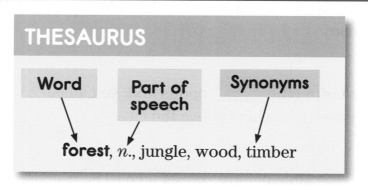

| Word | Part of speech | Synonyms |

forest, *n*., jungle, wood, timber

canopy *n*. umbrella, awning, foliage

leaf *n*. needle, frond, page

river *n*. stream, brook, creek

seed *n*. nut, kernel, stone

trunk *n*. chest, torso, stem

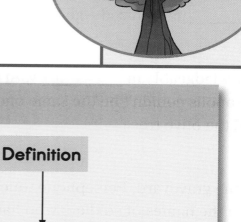

DICTIONARY

| Word | Part of speech | Definition |
| Pronunciation |

jungle *n*. \'jəŋ-gəl\ an impenetrable thicket or tangled mass of tropical vegetation

creek *n*. \'krēk\ a natural stream of water normally smaller than and often tributary to a river

frond *n*. \'fränd\ a large leaf (especially of a palm or fern) usually with many divisions

nut *n*. \'nət\ (1): a hard-shelled dry fruit with a separable rind or shell and interior kernel (2): the kernel of a nut

stem *n*. \'stem\ the main trunk of a plant

trunk *n*. \'trəŋk\ the main stem of a tree apart from limbs and roots—called also *bole*

umbrella *n*. \əm-'bre-lə\ device for protection from the rain or sun

Use clues from the thesaurus and dictionary to determine whether the new word can appropriately take the place of the synonym. If it can, draw a check mark. If it can't, draw an X.

○ The scientist fanned herself with the fallen palm **leaf** frond .

○ The Amazon **River** creek is the largest river in the world by volume.

○ The toucan lives in the rain forest **canopy** umbrella , the layer of forest in which leaves and branches create continuous shade.

Dictionary and Thesaurus

○ Tree **trunks** stems in the rain forest tend to be tall and bare, except for a collection of branches and leaves at the top.

○ Parrots use their strong jaws to break open shells and eat the **seeds** nuts inside.

Upon completion, add these stickers to your path on the map!

BONUS: What are two different definitions of the word "net"?

Now add this sticker to your map!

Summer Brain Quest: Between Grades 5 & 6

Moving Points

Find the products. (HINT: Remember to count the number of decimal places.)

Add Decimals

Upon completion, add this sticker to your path on the map!

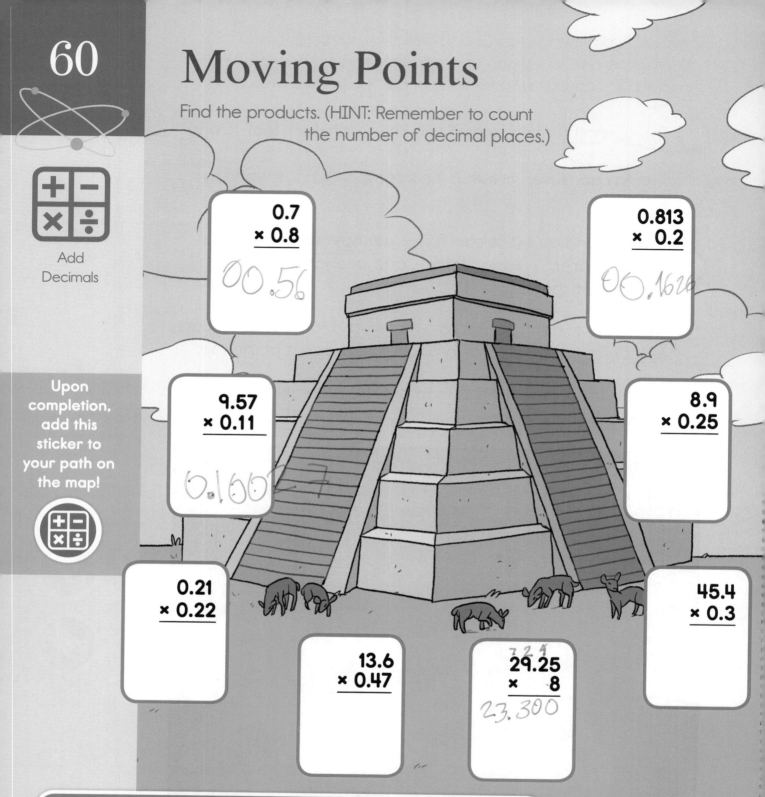

$$\begin{array}{r} 0.7 \\ \times\ 0.8 \\ \hline \end{array}$$
00.56

$$\begin{array}{r} 0.813 \\ \times\ 0.2 \\ \hline \end{array}$$
00.1626

$$\begin{array}{r} 9.57 \\ \times\ 0.11 \\ \hline \end{array}$$
0.16027

$$\begin{array}{r} 8.9 \\ \times\ 0.25 \\ \hline \end{array}$$

$$\begin{array}{r} 0.21 \\ \times\ 0.22 \\ \hline \end{array}$$

$$\begin{array}{r} 13.6 \\ \times\ 0.47 \\ \hline \end{array}$$

$$\begin{array}{r} 29.25 \\ \times\ 8 \\ \hline \end{array}$$
23.300

$$\begin{array}{r} 45.4 \\ \times\ 0.3 \\ \hline \end{array}$$

BONUS: Deer are native to many different countries throughout North, Central, and South America. If a scientist counted about 525,000 deer in Mexico and then multiplied that number by 0.001 to estimate the growth in population in one month, what would be the growth?

Now add this sticker to your map!

Level 4B complete!

Add this achievement sticker to your path…

…and move on to

Level 5B

on page 62!

Context Clues

START
LEVEL
5B
HERE!

Upon completion, add this sticker to your path on the map!

Brain Box

Context clues are pieces of information in a text that help you to determine the meanings of unfamiliar words or phrases.

Yo-ho-ho!

Read the passage from *Treasure Island*, by Robert Louis Stevenson. Then, based on context clues, underline the correct meaning for each word or phrase.

I remember him as if it were yesterday, as he came **plodding running / walking slowly** to the inn door, his sea-chest following behind him in a hand-barrow—a tall, strong, heavy, nut-brown man, his tarry pigtail falling over the shoulder of his **soiled dirty / shiny / blue** coat, his hands ragged and scarred, with black, broken nails, and the **sabre cut wound from a sword / tiger tattoo** across one cheek, a dirty, livid white. I remember him looking round the cover and whistling to himself as he did so, and then breaking out in that old sea-song that he sang so often afterwards:

"Fifteen men on the dead man's chest—
Yo-ho-ho, and a bottle of rum!"

in the high, old **tottering beautiful / unsteady** voice that seemed to have been tuned and broken at the capstan bars. Then he **rapped kicked / knocked** on the door with a bit of stick like a handspike that he carried, and when my father appeared, called roughly for a glass of rum. This, when it was brought to him, he drank slowly, like a **connoisseur an expert in matters of taste / a shipbuilder**, lingering on the taste and still looking about him at the cliffs and up at our signboard.

"This is a **handy cove nice location on the bay / ugly part of the country**," says he at length; "and a pleasant sittyated grog-shop. **Much company many customers / good weather**, mate?"

My father told him no, very little company, the more was the pity.

"Well, then," said he, "this is the **berth resting place / business** for me. . . ."

Solar Cookies

Read about Jada's engineering design project. Then answer the questions.

Engineering Design

Jada wanted to bake cookies but didn't want to heat up the house by using the oven. She decided to make a homemade solar oven. She knew that the oven would have to get very hot, and therefore would need to absorb and retain as much heat from the sun as possible. She cut off the lid of the pizza box and covered the inside with foil. That would reflect the heat of the sun onto the cookies. After dropping the cookie dough onto the foil, she covered the box with plastic wrap to trap the heat. Two hours later, the cookies were cooked on the outside but doughy inside. Jada thought too much heat was escaping: She needed a better-insulated box. She lined the box with foam and then also taped foil-lined cardboard on top of the foam. Finally, she substituted a sheet of glass for the flimsy plastic wrap. This time the cookies baked all the way through. Mmm . . . success is so delicious!

What is Jada trying to do?

_____

What does Jada know about the problem and solution?

_____

_____

What is Jada's first solution?

_____

How does that work?

_____

How does Jada improve her design?

_____

_____

Upon completion, add this sticker to your path on the map!

Brain Box

The process of **engineering design** is defining the problem, brainstorming and researching potential solutions, considering multiple ideas, developing a solution, testing the solution, and then refining the solution.

Diving for Denominators

Multiply each fraction by the denominator of the other fraction to find a common denominator. Then answer the questions.

Common
Denominators

Common
Denominators

Upon completion, add this sticker to your path on the map!

$\frac{1}{2}$ and $\frac{1}{3}$	$\frac{1}{2} = \frac{1 \times 3}{2 \times 3} =$	$\frac{1}{3} = \frac{1 \times 2}{3 \times 2} =$
$\frac{1}{3}$ and $\frac{2}{5}$	$\frac{1}{3} = \frac{1 \times}{3 \times} =$	$\frac{2}{5} = \frac{2 \times}{5 \times} =$
$\frac{3}{4}$ and $\frac{5}{12}$	$\frac{3}{4} = \frac{3 \times}{4 \times} =$	$\frac{5}{12} = \frac{5 \times}{12 \times} =$
$\frac{1}{2}$ and $\frac{3}{8}$	$\frac{1}{2} = \frac{1 \times}{2 \times} =$	$\frac{3}{8} = \frac{3 \times}{8 \times} =$
$\frac{5}{12}$ and $\frac{1}{6}$	$\frac{5}{12} = \frac{5 \times}{12 \times} =$	$\frac{1}{6} = \frac{1 \times}{6 \times} =$
$\frac{3}{4}$ and $\frac{5}{6}$	$\frac{3}{4} = \frac{3 \times}{4 \times} =$	$\frac{5}{6} = \frac{5 \times}{6 \times} =$

When you multiply the denominators, do you always find a common denominator? _____

By multiplying the two denominators, will you always get the least common denominator? _____

Brain Box

The **least common multiple** (LCM) of two numbers is the smallest number that is a multiple of both numbers.

The **least common denominator** (LCD) is the least common multiple of the denominators.

Sometimes the LCM is neither of the numbers.	Sometimes the LCM is one of the numbers.
Find the LCM of 2 and 3.	Find the LCM of 2 and 8.
Multiples of 2: 2, 4, 6, 8, 10 . . .	Multiples of 2: 2, 4, 6, 8, 10 . . .
Multiples of 3: 3, 6, 9, 12, 15 . . .	Multiples of 8: 8, 16, 24 . . .
The LCM is 6.	The LCM is 8.
The LCD of $\frac{1}{2}$ and $\frac{1}{3}$ is 6.	The LCD of $\frac{1}{2}$ and $\frac{1}{8}$ is 8.

Explorers

Complete the crossword puzzle about the Age of Exploration.

Age of Exploration

Brain Box

The Age of Exploration refers to the time from 1400 to 1600 when Europeans traveled the world to acquire raw materials, land, and other assets.

Upon completion, add this sticker to your path on the map!

Across

1 European newcomers carried a silent weapon: _____ from the Old World.

5 Spanish explorers could overcome native peoples because of new weapons technology such as _____ .

8 Explorers were able to determine direction in the open sea thanks to a Chinese invention: the magnetic _____ .

BONUS: Prior to the Age of Exploration, people had been crossing oceans in search of new lands for tens of thousands of years. Why might they have embarked on these long ocean journeys?

Down

1 During the Age of Exploration, many new navigational _____ made long sea journeys possible.

2 A new type of fast and maneuverable ship was the caravel, one of which was Columbus's _____ .

3 A mariner's astrolabe could be used to determine the ship's latitude based on the noon altitude of the _____ .

4 When Spanish explorers reached the Americas, they set out to _____ those who lived there.

6 _____ , long-extinct in North and South America, were also powerful assets to Spanish conquistadors on the battlefield.

7 Explorers could navigate from point to point using the Mercator projection, a flat _____ that shows where landmasses are in relation to each other.

Now add this sticker to your map!

_____

_____

Island Hopping

Add or subtract to color-code your map.

Adding and Subtracting Fractions and Mixed Numbers

$\frac{1}{2} + \frac{3}{12} =$

$\frac{1}{2} + \frac{3}{4} = \frac{2}{4} + \frac{3}{4} = \frac{5}{4} = 1\frac{1}{4}$

$\frac{15}{16} + \frac{1}{4} =$

$\frac{1}{2} + \frac{2}{3} =$

$\frac{9}{10} + \frac{1}{5} =$

$\frac{5}{8} + \frac{1}{4} =$

$\frac{5}{6} + \frac{3}{4} =$

$\frac{9}{16} + \frac{3}{4} =$

Brain Box

Improper fraction $\frac{5}{3} = 1\frac{2}{3}$ **Mixed number**	
Not simplest form $\frac{6}{8} = \frac{3}{4}$ **Simplest form** $1\frac{7}{6} = 2\frac{1}{6}$	

To add or subtract mixed numbers:

First, add or subtract the fractions. (Rewrite with common denominators, if necessary.) Then, add or subtract the whole numbers. Last, write your answer as a mixed number.

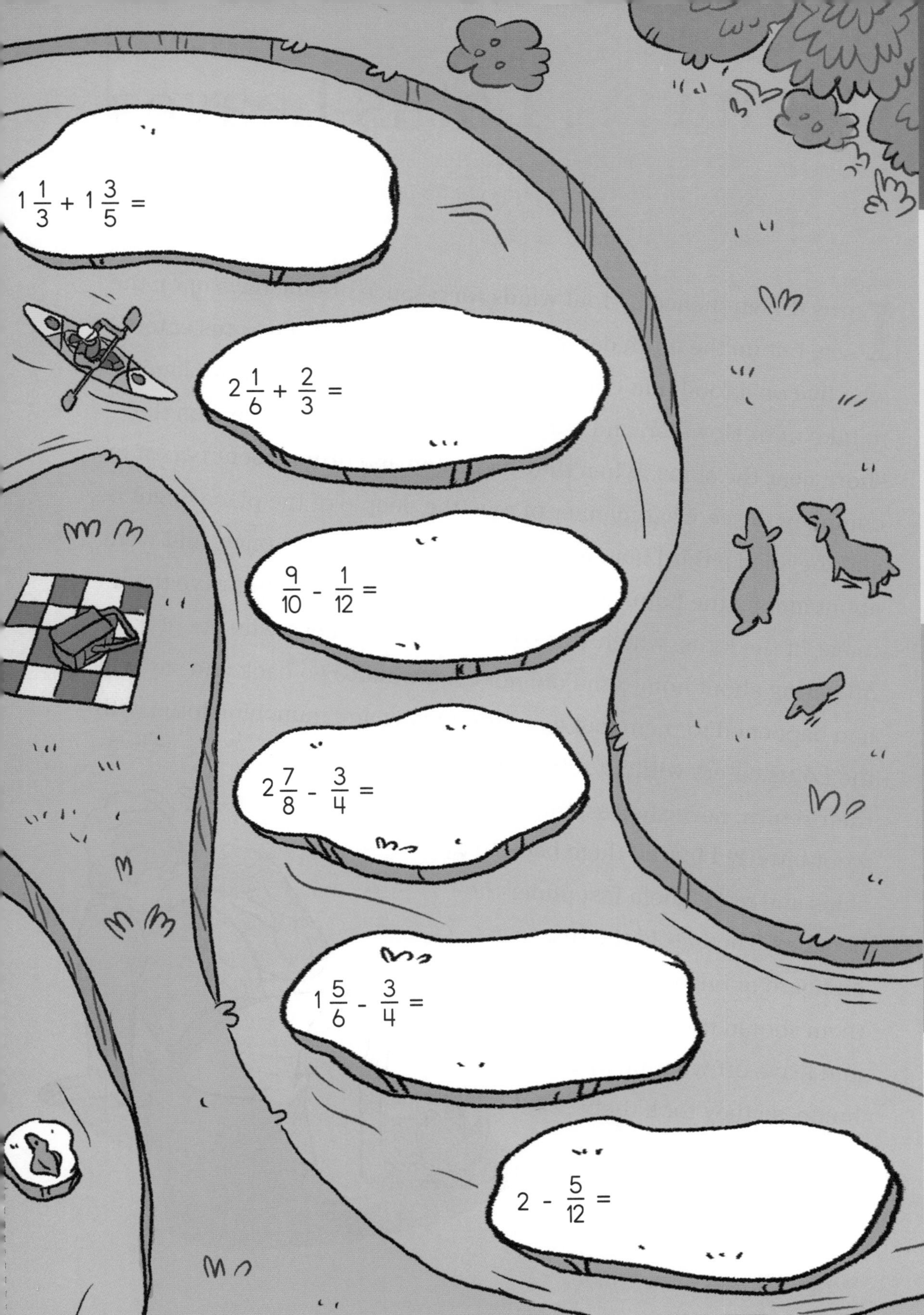

$1\frac{1}{3} + 1\frac{3}{5} =$

$2\frac{1}{6} + \frac{2}{3} =$

$\frac{9}{10} - \frac{1}{12} =$

$2\frac{7}{8} - \frac{3}{4} =$

$1\frac{5}{6} - \frac{3}{4} =$

$2 - \frac{5}{12} =$

Adding and
Subtracting
Fractions
and Mixed
Numbers

Upon
completion,
add these
stickers to
your path on
the map!

There are rare flowers on islands with answers
less than 1. Color those islands **pink**.

There are exotic animals on islands with answers
between 1 and 2. Color those islands **green**.

There is buried treasure on islands with answers
greater than 2. Color those islands **orange**.

Reading
Literature

Mmm . . . Lotus Leaves

Read the passage from *The Odyssey*. Then answer the questions.

I was driven thence by foul winds for a space of nine days upon the sea, but on the tenth day we reached the land of the Lotus-eaters, who live on a food that comes from a kind of flower. Here we landed to take in fresh water, and our crews got their mid-day meal on the shore near the ships. When they had eaten and drunk I sent two of my company to see what manner of men the people of the place might be, and they had a third man under them. They started at once, and went about among the Lotus-eaters, who did them no hurt, but gave them to eat of the lotus, which was so delicious that those who ate of it left off caring about home, and did not even want to go back and say what had happened to them, but were for staying and munching lotus with the Lotus-eaters without thinking further of their return; nevertheless, though they wept bitterly I forced them back to the ships and made them fast under the benches. Then I told the rest to go on board at once, lest any of them should taste of the lotus and leave off wanting to get home, so they took their places and smote the grey sea with their oars.

Brain Box

Literature is a written work with artistic merit, a designation often given after a work has stood the test of time. One such work, *The Odyssey* by the poet Homer, dates to 800 BCE. It's an epic poem about a war hero, Odysseus, who after the Trojan War travels to strange lands in the course of his journey home.

What happened to those who ate lotus?

_____

_____

_____

Which of the following is true of the Lotus-eaters? Underline one.

They jealously guard their lotus so that no one else will eat it.

They willingly share their lotus with others.

They are homesick.

Name a character from a book, movie, or TV show who, like a Lotus-eater, forgets his or her own goals and only wants to eat, relax, or have fun all the time. Explain your answer.

_____

_____

_____

Rewrite this story as though it happened to you and your family or friends during summer vacation. Describe how you got to the place, what it was like there, what food or activity made you not want to return home, and how you got back home.

_____

_____

_____

_____

_____

_____

_____

_____

_____

Reading Literature

Upon completion, add these stickers to your path on the map!

70

Multiplying
Fractions

A Bird in the Hand

Fill in the blanks. Then find the products and simplify if possible.

The beach conservation society roped off 4 sections of the beach to protect nesting birds. The birds nested in $\frac{2}{3}$ of each section. How many whole sections is $4 \times \frac{2}{3}$ equal to?

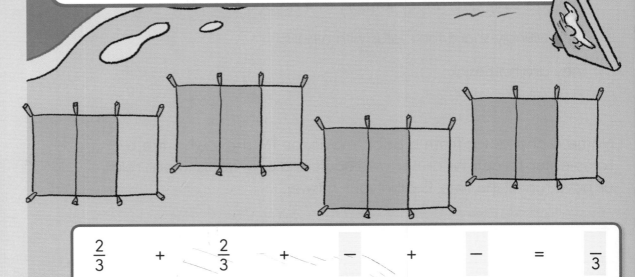

$$\frac{2}{3} + \frac{2}{3} + \boxed{} + \boxed{} = \frac{\boxed{}}{3}$$

$$4 \times \frac{2}{3} = \frac{4}{1} \times \frac{2}{3} = \frac{4 \times 2}{1 \times 3} = \frac{\boxed{}}{3} = \boxed{}\frac{\boxed{}}{3}$$

$5 \times \frac{2}{10} =$

$3 \times \frac{3}{8} =$

$4 \times \frac{3}{4} =$

$5 \times \frac{1}{3} =$

$7 \times \frac{5}{6} =$

$3 \times \frac{4}{10} =$

$10 \times \frac{1}{5} =$

$2 \times \frac{7}{12}$

$7 \times \frac{2}{5}$

Brain Box

To multiply a fraction times a whole number, write the whole number as a fraction with 1 as the denominator. Then multiply numerators, multiply denominators, and simplify.

Fill in the blanks. Then find the products and simplify if possible.

The beach conservation society found that some turtles lay their eggs in $\frac{1}{2}$ of a roped-off area. What part of a roped-off area has both birds' nests and turtle eggs?

The shaded and striped area is $\frac{}{}$ of the whole.

Multiplying Fractions

$$\frac{1}{2} \times \frac{2}{3} = \frac{1 \times 2}{2 \times 3} = \frac{}{} = \frac{}{}$$

$\frac{3}{8} \times \frac{1}{3} =$

$\frac{7}{16} \times \frac{1}{2} =$

$\frac{4}{10} \times \frac{2}{3} =$

$\frac{2}{5} \times \frac{1}{4} =$

$\frac{1}{6} \times \frac{5}{6} =$

$\frac{3}{4} \times \frac{3}{8} =$

$\frac{2}{5} \times \frac{7}{8} =$

$\frac{1}{3} \times \frac{1}{4} =$

$\frac{3}{10} \times \frac{2}{5} =$

Upon completion, add these stickers to your path on the map!

BONUS: A weather buoy showed the wind was blowing at 28 miles per hour. One hour later, the speed was $\frac{3}{4}$ of that. What was the wind speed one hour later?

Now add this sticker to your map!

Summer Brain Quest: Between Grades 5 & 6

Dive-in Restaurant

Read the chart. Then use the transitional words and phrases in the first column to fill in the blanks. (HINT: Some words can be used interchangeably.)

Transitional Words and Phrases

If you say . . .	You mean . . .
Also In addition Moreover Similarly	This thought will **add** to my previous thought.
Although Yet However On the other hand	This thought will **contrast** my previous thought.
For example For instance	This thought will **illustrate** my previous thought.
In other words Specifically	This thought will **clarify** my previous thought.

A Splashy New Restaurant

By: The Kid Critic

If you want to have fun at a restaurant, go to Swimmy's. You actually swim to your table! The chairs are all underwater. _____, your food arrives in a little boat. The boats travel on underwater

conveyor belts along the edge of the restaurant, sort of like water rides at amusement parks. One drawback is that the food can get a little wet. _____, my burger had been splashed, so I could not eat the bun. _____, my mom's fries were damp. _____, I think this was a malfunction in our food boat. When my mom mentioned the problem to a staff member, he took the boat out of the rotation. _____, I don't think this would happen on a second visit. Burger bun or no burger bun, the whole experience was unforgettable.

Level 5B complete!

Add this achievement sticker to your path...

...and move on to

Level 6

on page 94!

Earth's
Systems

START
LEVEL
5A
HERE!

Upon
completion,
add this
sticker to
your path on
the map!

Water, Water Everywhere

Read the passage. Then complete the diagram with words from the box.

The **hydrologic cycle** is the circulation of water through land, ocean, and atmosphere. **Evaporation** is the process of water from bodies of water and land being heated by the sun so that the water becomes vapor (gas) in the atmosphere. Through **transpiration**, leaves also emit water vapor into the atmosphere. Once water is a vapor, the gas cools and becomes liquid water droplets in a process called **condensation**. This is how clouds form. **Crystallization** is when the droplets freeze in cold conditions. **Precipitation** is when droplets fall as rain, snow, or ice. **Downhill flow** describes the movement of water downhill and ultimately into the ocean.

transpiration   evaporation   condensation
crystallization   precipitation   downhill flow

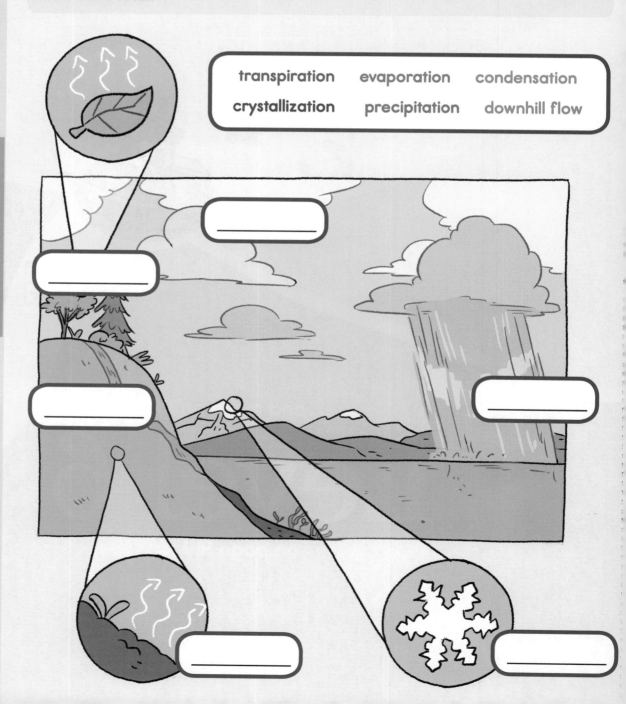

A Tense Situation

Read about the Vikings. Circle the inappropriate shifts in verb tense.

Verb Tense

Vikings were a seafaring people from Scandinavia who, from 800 to 1100 CE, raided Britain, other parts of Europe, and beyond, and ultimately settled in those lands. The Vikings' motive is simple: They desired wealth in the form of stolen riches and captured slaves. Before they set out to pillage distant nations, the Scandinavians had been trading iron and fur with closer European nations. From these trade partners, the Scandinavians (already adept sailors) learn how to build better ships. They also learned of the fractured feudal kingdoms in Britain and Europe—easy pickings for the Vikings.

The Vikings' first raids were on monasteries in Britain, which were left unguarded because most warriors left religious institutions alone. But the Vikings are not Christians and have no respect for such institutions. They soon settled in Scotland and Ireland, launching their attacks and trading enterprises from there. They later came to reside in Europe, Iceland, and Greenland. Eventually, Scandinavia was converted to Christianity, and the Christianized Viking culture merges with the cultures of its adopted lands.

Upon completion, add this sticker to your path on the map!

Write the incorrect verbs in the correct tense.

_____

_____

_____

_____

Brain Box

A story can have both **past** and **present tense**, but there must be a reason for the shift.

Example: I live in Chicago. My family moved here last June.

The narrator presently lives in Chicago, but he or she moved there in the past.

Lunch Break

Draw lines to represent sharing sandwiches. Color the portion one person gets.

If 1 sandwich is shared equally by 2 people, how much does each person get?

$1 \div 2 =$ ____
Each person gets ____ of a sandwich.

If 1 sandwich is shared equally by 3 people, how much does each person get?

$1 \div 3 =$ ____
Each person gets ____ of a sandwich.

If 2 sandwiches are shared equally by 3 people, how much does each person get?

$2 \div 3 =$ ____
Each person gets ____ of a sandwich.

If 3 sandwiches are shared equally by 2 people, how much does each person get?

$3 \div 2 =$ ____
Each person gets ____ half portions of a sandwich, which is ____.

Map It!

Study the political map of North America. Then color the countries according to the directions.

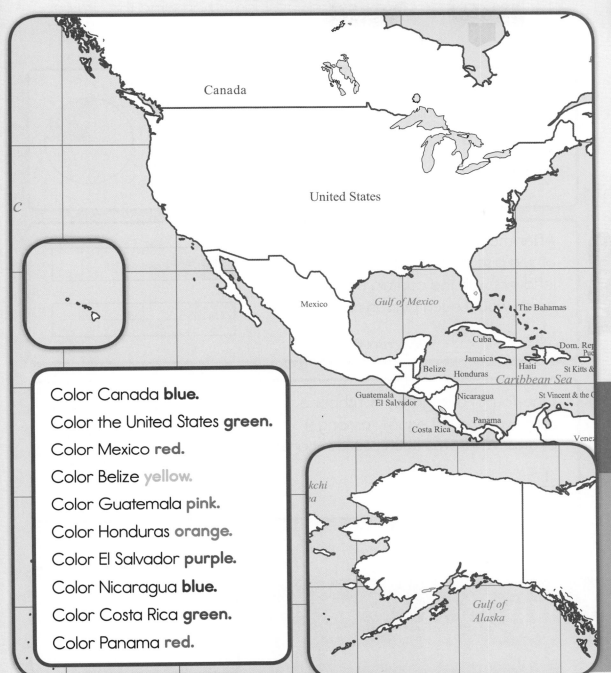

Color Canada **blue.**

Color the United States **green.**

Color Mexico **red.**

Color Belize yellow.

Color Guatemala **pink.**

Color Honduras **orange.**

Color El Salvador **purple.**

Color Nicaragua **blue.**

Color Costa Rica **green.**

Color Panama **red.**

Upon completion, add this sticker to your path on the map!

Brain Box

A **political map** shows the boundaries of countries, states or provinces, or counties. It also may show major cities and bodies of water.

BONUS: If a frog is found in Australia that shares a distant ancestor with a frog in South America, what could be the explanation (assuming that the frog species cannot survive in salt water)?

_____

_____

_____

Now add this sticker to your map!

Pirates in the Pantry

Circle the correct picture for each problem. Then write the answer.

Dividing with Fractions

If 4 pirate cooks divided $\frac{1}{2}$ pound of dried beans equally, how much would each cook get?

$\frac{1}{2} \div 4 =$ _____ pound(s)

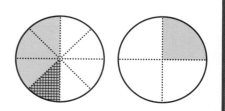

After mealtime, there was $\frac{1}{3}$ kilogram of sea biscuits left. If a cook shared the leftovers with the captain equally, how much would each person receive?

$\frac{1}{3} \div 2 =$ _____ kilogram(s)

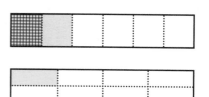

One-fourth of a gallon of fishbone soup was shared equally among 4 pirates. What was each pirate's share?

$\frac{1}{4} \div 4 =$ _____ gallon(s)

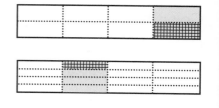

Find the quotient.

$\frac{1}{5} \div 5 =$

$\frac{1}{8} \div 2 =$

$\frac{1}{6} \div 3 =$

Brain Box

When you are dividing a fraction by a whole number, you are dividing a part of a whole into smaller parts, so the number gets smaller.

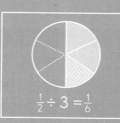

$\frac{1}{2} \div 3 = \frac{1}{6}$

When dividing a whole number by a fraction, you are dividing a whole number by a part of a whole. So the number gets bigger.

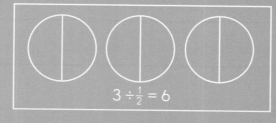

$3 \div \frac{1}{2} = 6$

Draw lines in the pictures to model each problem. Then write the answer.

The chef made 4 pickled-beet pizzas, and equally divided each into eighths. How many slices of pizza did he make?

$4 \div \frac{1}{8} = $ _____ slice(s)

The chef divided 5 gallons of sauerkraut into one-sixth gallon portions. How many portions of sauerkraut were there?

$5 \div \frac{1}{6} = $ _____ portion(s)

Ten pounds of salt pork were divided into shares that were $\frac{1}{4}$ pound each. How many shares were there?

$10 \div \frac{1}{4} = $ _____ share(s)

Find the quotient.

$4 \div \frac{1}{5} = $

$9 \div \frac{1}{2} = $

$7 \div \frac{1}{10} = $

Division with Fractions

Upon completion, add these stickers to your path on the map!

Brain Box

When dividing a fraction by a whole number (or vice versa), first insert 1 as the denominator for the whole number (this doesn't change the number because any number divided by 1 is itself). Then flip the second fraction and multiply the fractions.

$\frac{2}{3} \div 5$

$\frac{2}{3} \div \frac{5}{1}$

$\frac{2}{3} \times \frac{1}{5} = \frac{2}{15}$

$5 \div \frac{2}{3}$

$\frac{5}{1} \div \frac{2}{3}$

$\frac{5}{1} \times \frac{3}{2} = \frac{15}{2} = 7\frac{1}{2}$

What a Character!

Read the excerpt from *Alice's Adventures in Wonderland* by Lewis Carroll. Then answer the questions.

Alice was beginning to get very tired of sitting by her sister on the bank, and of having nothing to do: once or twice she had peeped into the book her sister was reading, but it had no pictures or conversations in it, "and what is the use of a book," thought Alice, "without pictures or conversations?"

So she was considering in her own mind (as well as she could, for the hot day made her feel very sleepy and stupid), whether the pleasure of making a daisy-chain would be worth the trouble of getting up and picking the daisies, when suddenly a White Rabbit with pink eyes ran close by her.

There was nothing so very remarkable in that; nor did Alice think it so very much out of the way to hear the Rabbit say to itself, "Oh dear! Oh dear! I shall be late!" (when she thought it over afterwards, it occurred to her that she ought to have wondered at this, but at the time it all seemed quite natural); but when the Rabbit actually took a watch out of its waistcoat-pocket, and looked at it, and then hurried on, Alice started to her feet, for it flashed across her mind that she had never before seen a rabbit with either a waistcoat-pocket, or a watch to take out of it, and burning with curiosity, she ran across the field after it, and fortunately was just in time to see it pop down a large rabbit-hole under the hedge.

In another moment down went Alice after it, never once considering how in the world she was to get out again.

The rabbit-hole went straight on like a tunnel for some way, and then dipped suddenly down, so suddenly that Alice had not a moment to think about stopping herself before she found herself falling down a very deep well.

Either the well was very deep, or she fell very slowly, for she had plenty of time as she went down to look about her and to wonder what was going to happen next. First, she tried to look down and make out what she was coming to, but it was too dark to see anything; then she looked at the sides of the well, and noticed that they were filled with cupboards and book-shelves; here and there she saw maps and pictures hung upon pegs. She took down a jar from one of the shelves as she passed; it was labelled ORANGE MARMALADE, but to her great disappointment it was empty: she did not like to drop the jar for fear of killing somebody, so managed to put it into one of the cupboards as she fell past it.

Write two adjectives that the author uses to describe how Alice is feeling at the beginning of the passage.

_____

In this passage, "stupid" doesn't mean unintelligent. Based on context clues, what could it mean instead?

_____

What does the detail of Alice picking up the marmalade jar and checking its contents NOT tell you about her character?

> She is prone to panic.
>
> She is curious.
>
> She likes marmalade.

What does the detail of Alice setting the marmalade in the cupboard rather than dropping it tell you about her character?

_____

What traits does Alice have that make her a good character for an adventure story?

_____

Judging from the introduction, what is a likely character arc for Alice?

> Having lost everything she loved, Alice transforms into a warrior motivated only by revenge.
>
> In a rut, Alice tries desperately to better her situation through hard work and a fresh perspective.
>
> Faced with a world that doesn't make sense, Alice learns just how brave and capable she really is.

Which best describes the narration in this passage?

> **Third-person limited:** The narrator sees things through the eyes of a character and knows only the thoughts and feelings of that character.
>
> **Third-person omniscient:** The narrator sees all, including the thoughts and feelings of characters, and realities that the characters may not realize.

BONUS: Write three sentences about a person at a beach from a seagull's point of view.

Now add this sticker to your map!

_____
_____
_____

Brain Box

Elements of **literature** include theme, conflict, setting, voice, point of view, symbolism, and strong characters.

Scottish Solutions

Write an equation to solve each problem, and label each answer.

A family went on 3 short hikes. Each was $\frac{7}{10}$ kilometers long. How many kilometers did the family hike in all?

Equation:	Answer:

A group of tourists wants to visit a castle $15\frac{3}{4}$ kilometers away. They bike for $6\frac{1}{2}$ kilometers and then stop for lunch. How many more kilometers do they still need to bike?

Equation:	Answer:

A family had 4 sandwiches to share among 3 people, so each sandwich was cut into thirds. How many sandwiches did each person eat?

Equation:	Answer:

Bagpipers perform for 8 minutes. The spectators interrupted with applause every $\frac{1}{2}$ minute. Including the final applause, how many times were the bagpipers applauded?

Equation:

Answer:

There are 5 different parts of the castle tour. Each part is $\frac{5}{6}$-hour long. What is the total amount of time of the tour?

Equation:

Answer:

Upon completion, add these stickers to your path on the map!

A recipe for Scottish porridge uses $\frac{1}{10}$ kilogram of oats to make 2 servings. How many kilograms of oats are in each serving?

Equation:

Answer:

A recipe for Scottish scones requires $\frac{1}{3}$ cup of butter to make 12 scones. If you want to make 24 scones, how many cups of butter will you need?

Equation:

Answer:

BONUS: Nessie's Nibbles are sold at the Loch Ness Monster Look-Out Snack Bar. If a family of 3 shares $\frac{1}{2}$ pound of the snacks, how many pounds of nibbles will each person eat?

Now add this sticker to your map!

Summer Brain Quest: Between Grades 5 & 6

Evolution

Dog Days

Unscramble the words to complete the sentences about dog evolution.

If you were new to planet Earth, you'd never believe that a Great Dane and pug were members of the same **pescise.** _____

How is it that dog breeds differ so greatly in their **ormpohogyl** (physical appearance)? _____

Scientists believe that canids, which include dogs, wolves, and foxes, have certain **enges** that mutate quickly. _____

This is why you find such interesting **rattis**—the large ears of bat-eared foxes or the long legs of maned wolves, for instance—among wild canids. _____

Many scientists believe all domestic dogs **voledev** from one canid species: the South Asian wolf. _____

People began **rebeding** dogs by selecting certain dogs with the same helpful traits to mate. _____

The gene **tumanoti** that caused short legs was selected for many reasons, including the ability the dogs would have to pursue burrowing animals. _____

The evolvability (ability to adapt and evolve genetically) of dogs makes them ideal for **modtesitacino.** _____

Scientists believe foxes could be domesticated over many **egenaritons,** just as dogs once were. _____

Upon completion, add this sticker to your path on the map!

Brain Box

With **domesticated** animals, selective **breeding** speeds the process of evolution, and they can be bred to create specific **traits**. Dog breeds vary greatly in their **morphology** (physical appearance) because their **genes** are more prone to mutations. So dogs can look very different from each other but still belong to the same **species.**

BONUS: In rare instances, people have monkeys for pets. Yet monkeys are not domesticated. What do you think is the difference between a pet and a domesticated animal?

_____
_____
_____
_____
_____

Now add this sticker to your map!

Level 5A complete!

Add this achievement sticker
to your path…

…and move on to

Level 6

on page 94!

Volume

START LEVEL **5C** HERE!

Upon completion, add this sticker to your path on the map!

Building Blocks

How many cubes of each size will it take to fill each tower? Write the volume. (HINT: If necessary, convert measurements before calculating.)

 This cube is 1 foot long on each side.
Volume = 1 cubic (ft³)

 This cube is 1 yard (3 feet) long on each side.
Volume = 1 cubic yard (yd³)

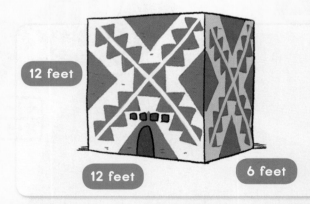

9 feet 6 feet 6 feet

Volume = _____ ft³

Volume = _____ yd³

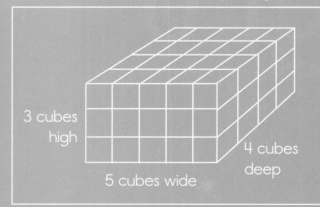

12 feet 12 feet 6 feet

Volume = _____ ft³

Volume = _____ yd³

Brain Box

Volume is the form of measurement used for solid figures. It can be measured by the number of cubes that will fill up a box-shaped figure.

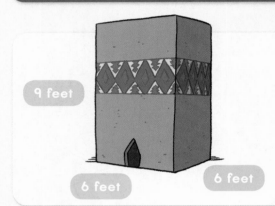

3 cubes high
5 cubes wide
4 cubes deep

The bottom layer will have 5 x 4 or 20 cubes.

The box is 3 cubes high, so there are 3 layers.

20 + 20 + 20 = 3 x 20 = 60 cubes in all.

The box is 60 cubic units.

You can write cubic units as units³.

Be an Illustrator

Choose from one of the prompts below. Then write and draw the first scene of your story as a graphic novel.

While riding through the forest, I happened upon another rider who looked like my twin. Both of us stopped in our tracks and then…

The new high-powered telescope allowed us to finally see the exoplanet orbiting the red dwarf star Kepler-186 in detail. As predicted, it was very similar to Earth, except for one shocking difference…

The decaying dugout canoe floated unanchored. Without stopping to think, I ran and leapt into it. The moment I landed, the canoe looked brand-new, and I was surrounded by…

Visual Elements

Upon completion, add this sticker to your path on the map!

Brain Box

Visual elements contribute to the meaning, tone, or beauty of an illustrated story or graphic novel.

Shrunken Solar System

If the solar system was shrunken so that 1 inch represented 100,000 miles, then the sun and planets would be the sizes of these familiar objects and would be the following distances apart.

Study the model solar system. Then answer the questions.

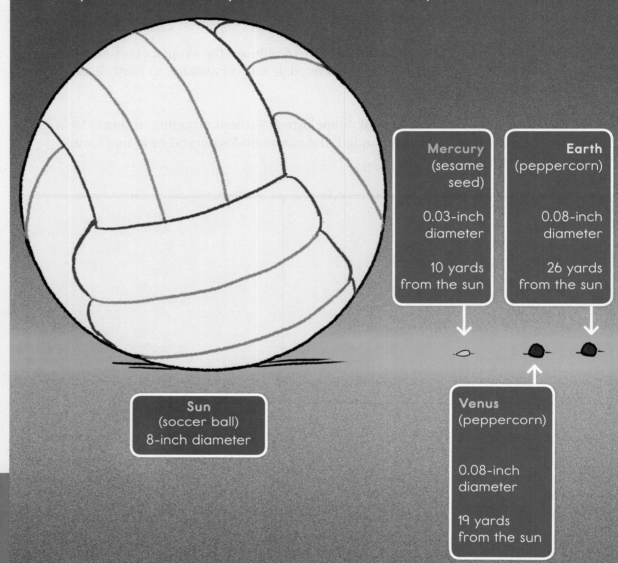

Mercury
(sesame seed)

0.03-inch diameter

10 yards from the sun

Earth
(peppercorn)

0.08-inch diameter

26 yards from the sun

Sun
(soccer ball)
8-inch diameter

Venus
(peppercorn)

0.08-inch diameter

19 yards from the sun

Brain Box

The **solar system** consists of the sun, eight planets, their many moons, and a plethora of dwarf planets and asteroids. All of these orbit around the sun because of its gravitational pull.

Which two planets are the smallest?

_____

Which planet is closest to the sun?

_____

Which planet is farthest from the sun?

_____

Upon completion, add these stickers to your path on the map!

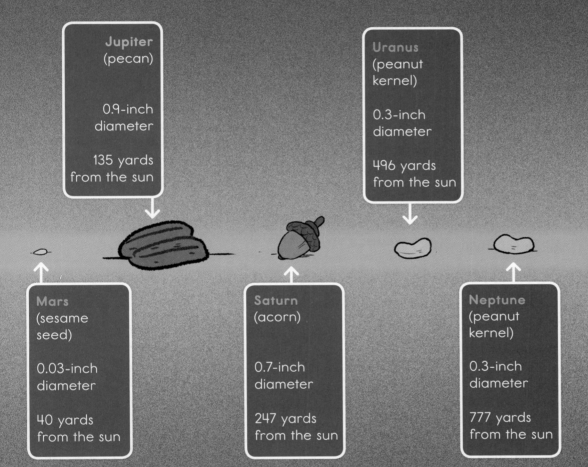

Jupiter
(pecan)

0.9-inch
diameter

135 yards
from the sun

Uranus
(peanut
kernel)

0.3-inch
diameter

496 yards
from the sun

Mars
(sesame
seed)

0.03-inch
diameter

40 yards
from the sun

Saturn
(acorn)

0.7-inch
diameter

247 yards
from the sun

Neptune
(peanut
kernel)

0.3-inch
diameter

777 yards
from the sun

Venus has been called Earth's evil twin because of its similar size and makeup but extreme heat during the day. What might be one reason that it gets much hotter than Earth?

_____

NASA aims to send humans to Mars by the 2030s. Why might this be the chosen planet to visit?

_____

_____

Ice Cold

Read the two informational texts about ice fishing.
Then answer the questions.

Ice Fishing Safety Rules

The creaking and cracking of lake ice as it fuses heralds the start of ice fishing season. Whether it's your first or fiftieth season on the ice, it's important to review the safety rules.

Ice must be a certain depth to hold weight. For individual walkers, ice must be 4 to 5 inches deep. For groups, the ice should be 7 to 8 inches deep. River ice must be 10 inches deep for safe walking. To safely drive on ice, an 18-inch depth is absolutely necessary.

Of course, 10 inches of ice in one spot doesn't mean the ice is safe everywhere. As the water depth increases, ice forms later, so test the depth as you proceed. Avoid areas with underwater springs, patches of snow, or objects frozen in the lake, which can all cause thin ice. Also, know that when the temperature rises above freezing for six or more hours in a day, ice conditions may change.

If you do fall through the ice, stay calm. Face the direction from which you approached. Climb onto the ice. Once out of the water, do not walk, as you could risk falling through again. Roll to land, change into dry clothes, and seek medical help. If a friend falls through the ice, do not run to his or her aid, as you could also fall in. Throw a rope or similar item to the friend instead. Help your friend into dry clothes and seek medical aid.

Sadly, many seasoned fishermen have lost their lives due to a single safety mistake. "Better safe than sorry" isn't just a saying. It should be a way of life for ice fishermen.

Ice Cold Fishing!

This winter break, I went ice fishing with my cousins in Minnesota. Their winters are much colder than ours here in Georgia, but the funny thing is, they are always outside. They skate, hike, and cross-country ski, but their favorite thing to do is to go ice fishing.

I was nervous to step onto the ice. What if it broke? My uncle chiseled a hole in the ice and dropped in the tip of a tape measure. The ice was 16 inches thick. He said that was twice as thick as necessary for a group of people walking on a lake. I cautiously stepped out onto it. As we got farther out onto the ice, I was struck by how quiet things were. Just then, I heard a loud creak. "Don't worry," my uncle said. "That's just the ice fusing together. It's not breaking, it's getting stronger."

We finally reached our "lucky spot." My uncle drilled some holes in the ice with this giant corkscrew-looking thing called an auger. He handed each of my cousins and me a jig—a rod for ice fishing. We attached lures. Then we each went to a hole. My cousin Dane showed me how to move the jig so that the lure spun through the water, attracting fish. All the sudden, I felt a tug. "Pull up!" said Dane. When I did, the jig barely moved.

Dane stared with wide eyes, and then said, "Finn's got a keeper!"

Soon my cousins had surrounded me, coaching me to pull this way and that. Finally, I reeled it in. A huge bass was staring me in the eye.

I reached into the icy water and grabbed the fish by the mouth!

Ouch—the water was bone-chilling. I lifted the bass out—it was a six pounder! My uncle snapped a photo, and then we threw it back in because we were catching and releasing. I'll never forget my first catch! If you can handle the cold too, I definitely recommend ice fishing!

What is the main idea of the first text?

_____

Write three details from the text that support the main idea.

_____

_____

_____

What is a synonym for "heralds" in the first paragraph of the first text?

discourages

cautions against

shouts

indicates

In the last paragraph of the first text, what does "seasoned" mean?

experienced

flavored

brave

ignorant

What information do both texts contain?

A fish should be pulled out of the water with one's bare hands.

Fish should be caught and released.

Ice on a lake must be 8 inches deep for a group walking on a lake.

Wet gloves will freeze.

Which of the following is an accurate comparison of the structure of the two texts?

"Ice Fishing Safety Rules" describes events chronologically, whereas "Ice Cold Fishing!" compares and contrasts two things.

"Ice Fishing Safety Rules" states problems and solutions, whereas "Ice Cold Fishing!" describes events chronologically.

Upon
completion,
add these
stickers to
your path on
the map!

Go on a
KEY
QUEST
on page 134
to retrieve

Cool Characters

Imagine that you are either a yeti (a large, hairy creature with humanlike traits) who encounters a human, or a boy or girl who encounters a yeti. Describe your character in the third person (he, she), and be as specific as possible.

What does the character look like?

_____

_____

Why is the character trekking through the snowy mountains?

_____

_____

Is he or she alone? Is he or she lost?

_____

_____

How does he or she respond to seeing the human or yeti?

_____

_____

What does he or she want from the person or yeti?

_____

How will he or she get it?

_____

_____

Level 5C complete!

Add this achievement sticker to your path…

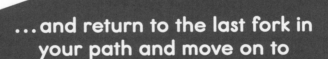

…and return to the last fork in your path and move on to

Level 5A

on page 74!

Volume

Ship Your Souvenirs

Find the volume of each prism.

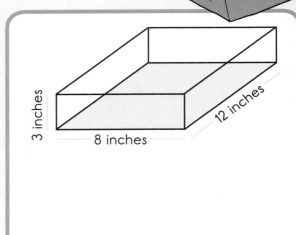

Upon completion, add this sticker to your path on the map!

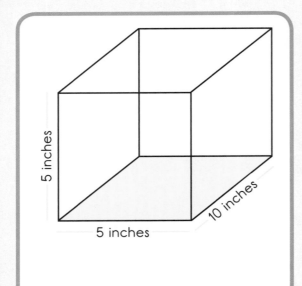

5 inches

5 inches

10 inches

3 inches

8 inches

12 inches

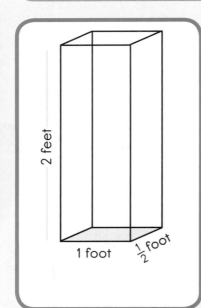

2 feet

1 foot

½ foot

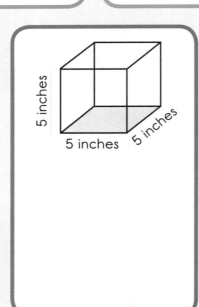

5 inches

5 inches

5 inches

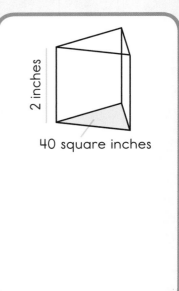

2 inches

40 square inches

⅓ foot

⅔ square feet

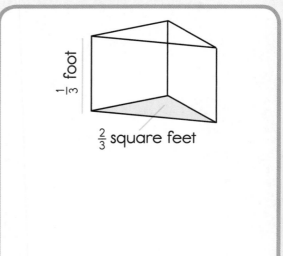

Brain Box

The volume of a prism can be found by multiplying the area of the base **B** times the height **h**.

When the base is a rectangle, the area of the base is length times width, therefore:

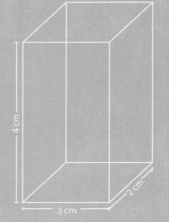

4 cm

3 cm

2 cm

$$V = B \times h$$
$$V = l \times w \times h$$
$$V = 2 \times 3 \times 4 = 24 \text{ cm}^3$$

Puzzle Break Time

Find the volume of each prism.
Then use the number of cubic units to solve the riddle.

Volume

l = 17 units
w = 3 units
h = 4 units

V = _____ units³

l = 8 units
w = 5 units
h = 8 units

V = _____ units³

l = 15 units
w = 10 units
h = 2 units

V = _____ units³

l = 3 units
w = 3 units
h = 19 units

V = _____ units³

l = 8 units
w = 8 units
h = 8 units

V = _____ units³

l = 20 units
w = 4 units
h = 8 units

V = _____ units³

l = 22 units
w = 18 units
h = 1 unit

V = _____ units³

l = 6 units
w = 6 units
h = 9 units

V = _____ units³

Upon completion, add this sticker to your path on the map!

Riddle:

What did the parrot's answering machine say when she was on vacation?

___ ___ ___ ___ - ___ ___ ___
512   204   396   324   640   204   300

___ ___ ___ ___ !
171   320   171   324

Physical Maps

Africa

Study the physical map of Africa. Then follow the directions to label the map with the bold names of features.

Madagascar is the largest island off the coast of Africa.

The **Mediterranean Sea** separates Africa and Europe.

The **Strait of Gibraltar** is the narrow passage between Morocco (in Africa) and Spain (in Europe) that leads from the **Atlantic Ocean** to the Mediterranean Sea.

The **Sahara Desert**, the largest nonpolar desert in the world, spans northern Africa.

Lake Victoria, one of Africa's many great lakes, is the second-largest freshwater lake in the world and the largest in Africa.

The **Nile** flows from Lake Victoria, creates a fertile valley in the Sahara, and continues north toward the Mediterranean Sea.

The **Red Sea** lies between Africa and the **Arabian Peninsula**.

The body of water between Africa and Madagascar is the **Mozambique Channel**.

The headwaters of the Nile are in **Egypt** and the highlands of **Ethiopia**.

The country farthest to the south is **South Africa**.

Lesotho is a country located entirely within the country of South Africa.

The **Indian Ocean** is to the east of Africa, and the Atlantic Ocean is to the West. The two oceans meet to the south of Africa.

BONUS: From 11,000 to 5,000 years ago, the Sahara Desert wasn't much of a desert at all. Cave paintings show that during this time people hunted wild game and then raised cattle, sheep, and goats in the once-lush grassland. The practice of raising animals spread from this region throughout the continent. What inference can be made from this?

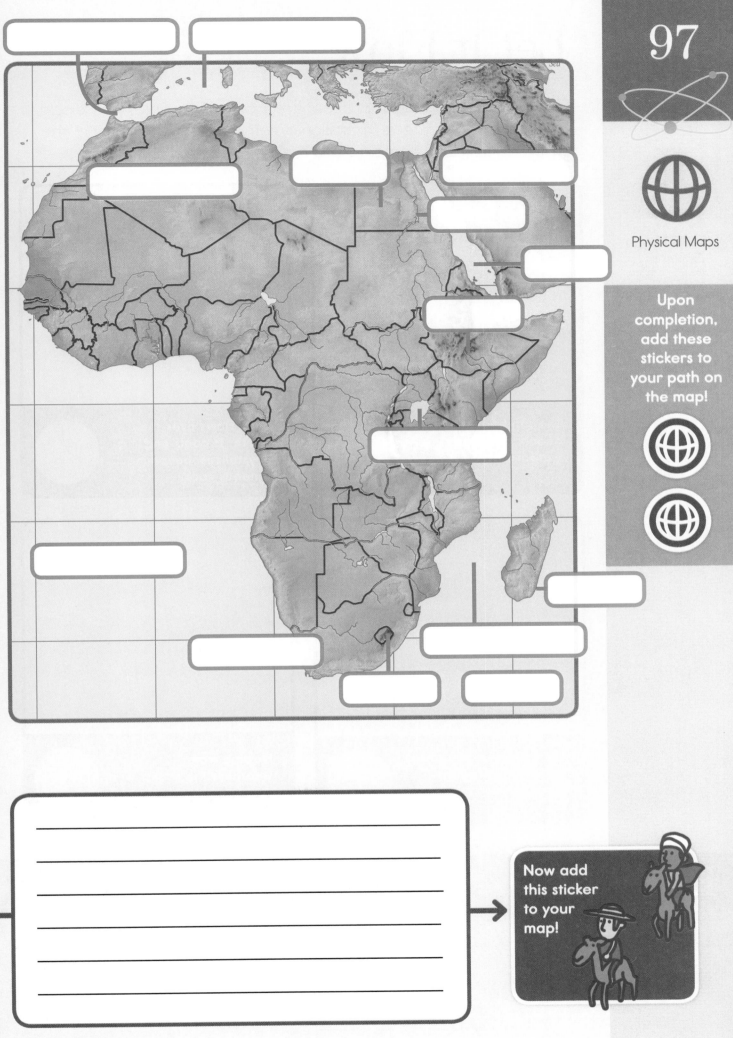

Physical Maps

Upon completion, add these stickers to your path on the map!

Now add this sticker to your map!

Let It Flow

Draw a picture for each process described. Then write R if it is part of the rock and mineral formation system. Write W if it is part of the water cycle. (HINT: Some can be both.)

The sun heats the ocean, and water evaporates.

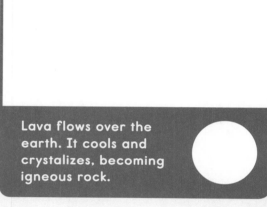

Lava flows over the earth. It cools and crystalizes, becoming igneous rock.

Water vapor condenses, and water droplets form clouds.

Flowing water weathers the rocks.

Brain Box

Energy from the sun and Earth's hot interior set in motion the **flow of energy** and **cycling of matter** that make up all **Earth processes**. A group of processes make up a **system,** and these systems **interact**. For instance, the system of mineral and rock formation includes the processes of melting, crystallization, weathering, deformation, and sedimentation. The water cycle is comprised of the processes of evaporation, transpiration, condensation, crystallization, precipitation, and downhill flow. These systems interact in many ways, including the weathering of rocks caused by the downhill flow of water.

As sediment piles up, sedimentary rock forms.

Some sedimentary rock is pushed down into Earth's hot core, where it melts.

Magma rises through Earth's rock layers, resulting in a volcano.

Rainwater carries sediment from the rocks downhill to the ocean, where it is deposited.

Upon completion, add these stickers to your path on the map!

BONUS: Rivers, lakes, and oceans deposit nutrient-rich sediment—silt, clay, sand, etc.—on their shores. How does a plant like a palm rely on this process for growth?

_____

_____

_____

_____

_____

Now add this sticker to your map!

Opinion
Writing

What Do YOU Think?

Choose one of the prompts. Then state your opinion in your own words and brainstorm five facts or logical arguments to support that opinion. If needed, consult a reliable source, such as the website of a museum, newspaper, government entity, or university.

 The city is putting in a new park just in time for summer, but it will have only ONE of the following: a swimming pool, goldfish pond, or skateboarding park. It should have a _____.

In the fall, your school is adding a new item to the lunch menu. It should be _____.

Brain Box

An **opinion piece** states a point of view and backs it up with facts and logical arguments.

 The most important thing for a student to do during summer vacation is (choose one) read/exercise/relax/visit new places/spend extra time with friends and family because _____.

Many employers won't hire summer workers younger than 15. If it were up to me, _____.

Your opinion in your own words_____

_____

Five supporting facts and/or logical arguments

1 _____

2 _____

3 _____

4 _____

5 _____

Write your opinion piece. Begin by stating your position. Then present your facts and arguments in a logical sequence. Use transition words and phrases such as **in addition, also, however, on the other hand,** and **for instance.** End with a concluding statement.

Opinion
Writing

Upon
completion,
add these
stickers to
your path on
the map!

_____

_____

_____

_____

_____

_____

_____

_____

_____

_____

_____

_____

_____

_____

Brain Box

A **concluding statement** sums up what was said in the paragraph and explains why it is important in a larger sense. Example: As nutritious as it is delicious, eggplant Parmesan would not only be a great new school lunch item, it would make kids want to try other new vegetables outside of school, too.

Rain Forest Ratios

Look at the picture and fill in the blanks to explain the ratio.

Ratio

Upon completion, add this sticker to your path on the map!

Brain Box

A **ratio** compares two quantities by division.

You can compare part to part, part to whole, or whole to part.

For example: In the string of letters **XXOOO**, the ratio of Xs to Os is 2 to 3. The ratio can also be written 2:3 or $\frac{2}{3}$.

The ratio of Xs to the total is 2 to 5, 2:5 or $\frac{2}{5}$.

The ratio of the total to Os is 5 to 3, 5:3 or $\frac{5}{3}$.

The ratio of toucans to anacondas is _____ : _____ because for every _____ toucans, there are _____ anacondas.

The ratio of blue morpho butterflies to anacondas is _____ : _____ because for every group of _____ blue morpho butterflies, there are _____ anacondas.

The ratio of spider monkeys to toucans is _____ : _____ because for every ____ spider monkeys, there are ____ toucans.

The ratio of jaguars to toucans is _____ : _____ because for very _____ jaguars, there are _____ toucans.

The ratio of jaguars to spider monkeys is _____ : _____ because for every _____ jaguars, there are _____ spider monkeys.

The ratio of spider monkeys to winged animals is _____ : _____ because there are _____ spider monkeys for every group of _____ winged animals.

Island Run

Writing
Narratives

Finish the story using as many transition words and phrases from the box as you can.

> Later   Farther down the beach   The next morning   Then
> Meanwhile, in the forest   Next   As night fell   First   Earlier

Shawanna was spending her summer at an elite cross-country camp in Thailand, where she was training with the best young runners in the world. Today, the runners had some downtime. They were going for a sailboat ride! The runners lounged and snacked, and before they knew it, a small island was in sight. Funny, a stopover wasn't on the itinerary. All of a sudden, *screech* . . . They weren't docking. They were crashing! As the ship ran aground, someone yelled the horrible news. The captain had keeled over and died! The runners had no idea where they were, and there were no grown-ups to help. They climbed off the boat and . . .

_____

_____

_____

_____

_____

_____

_____

_____

_____

_____

_____

_____

Brain Box

Transition words and phrases show that time has passed or the setting has changed. They also show the sequence of events.

Mongol
Empire

Grandpa Genghis

Read about Genghis Khan.

Genghis Khan means "Universal Ruler," an apt title for the man who built the largest land empire ever, starting completely from scratch. When Temujin (his given name) was born in 1162 CE, there was no Mongolian government. Instead, there were self-governing nomadic clans, which often kidnapped and stole from one another. Temujin's mother had been kidnapped by his father's clan; later his father was poisoned by a rival clan. When Temujin and his family were abandoned by their own clan, Temujin rose to become the head of his own household—by murdering his half-brother.

Temujin could have continued the tradition of fighting the other clans. Instead, he reached out to some of the leaders as allies. With their help, he attacked enemy clans, killing the leaders but absorbing other clan members into his fold. Drawing from his growing clan, Temujin established military units of ten and appointed the best leaders. He soon led a veritable super clan, which eventually became the nation of Mongolia. In 1206 CE, Temujin was named Genghis Khan, and he ruled over a nation of one million people.

As ruler, Genghis Khan outlawed some of the old clan practices, including kidnapping women and enslaving fellow Mongols. He also established a writing system, freedom of religion, and diplomatic immunity for ambassadors from other nations. His foreign relations, however, were far from peaceful. The Mongols began raiding other nations on horseback, seeking silk, minerals, and horses. The attacks were vicious, as was typical of military raids of the time, and cities were utterly destroyed. But Genghis Khan did spare the lives of religious leaders and skilled workers.

Genghis Khan died during a military campaign in 1227 CE, by then an old man. His empire extended from the East China Sea to the Caspian Sea. His grandson Kublai expanded it even farther into Eastern Europe, Persia, Tibet, southern China, and the Korean peninsula. Why Genghis Khan set out to conquer the world is a matter of debate. It may have been out of necessity, such as a shortage of food in Mongolia. Or it could have been the opposite—a time of plenty that led to more horses that could be deployed in battle. In that case, he may have set out to acquire more land, more subjects, and more riches for the same reason as other conquerors—because he wanted to and because he could.

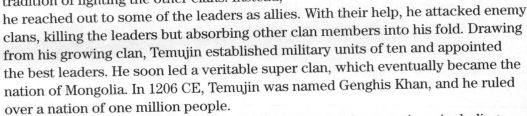

BONUS: If you encountered dry land where people lived in raised huts, what conclusion could you draw?

Pretend that you are Genghis Khan. Write a letter to your grandson explaining how you united Mongolia, and why you made decisions such as forging alliances in some cases and going to war in others. Lastly, give some possible reasons why you wanted to conquer the world.

Mongol Empire

Upon completion, add these stickers to your path on the map!

Now add this sticker to your map!

Fishing Coordinates

The table shows the number of fish caught over a number of hours. Write coordinate pairs and graph the coordinates.

Coordinate Pairs and Graphing

Hours	Fish Caught	
2	5	→ (2,5)
4	10	→ _____
6	15	→ _____
8	20	→ _____

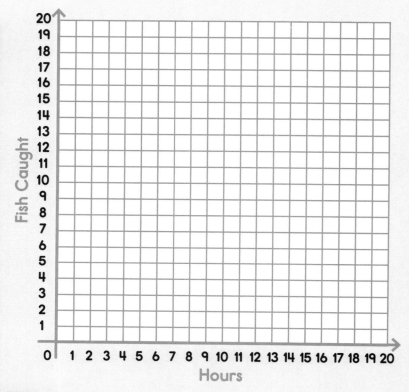

Brain Box

The corresponding numbers of two sequences of numbers can be written as **ordered pairs** or **coordinate pairs**.

0, 1, 2, 3, 4
0, 2, 4, 6, 8
can be paired and written as
(0, 0) (1, 2) (2, 4) (3, 6) (4, 8).

Then they can be **graphed** as points on a grid. The **x-axis** goes across. The **y-axis** goes up and down. The first number in the pair represents the **x coordinate**, and the second number represents the **y coordinate (x, y)**.

To graph a coordinate pair, go across x number of squares and go up y number of squares.

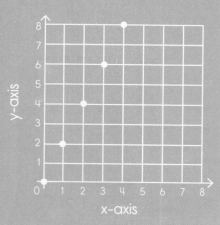

Notice that the points on the graph move up two squares for every one square they move over.

Monster Coordinates

Write the coordinates of each fish.

blue fish _____   green fish _____   orange fish _____   pink fish _____

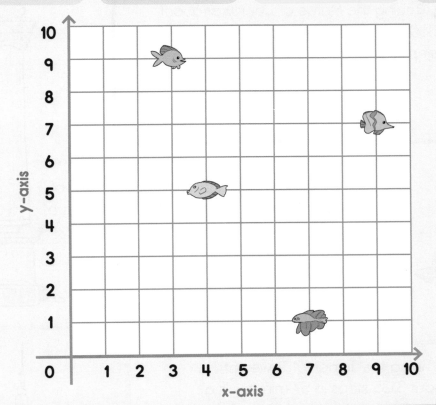

Coordinate Pairs and Graphing

Upon completion, add these stickers to your path on the map!

Why is the order of the coordinates in a coordinate pair important? Draw a fish at (1, 7) and use it to explain your answer.

_____

_____

Plot the location of each sea monster and draw it on the coordinate plane.
A furry fish is at (1, 9).
An island-size turtle is at (3, 7).
A gigantic octopus is at (5, 5).
A many-headed monster is at (7, 3).

Describe the pattern of points. _____

_____

Bigfoot is so hot that he goes for a swim. The location of Bigfoot continues the pattern of points above. What are the coordinates for Bigfoot? Plot the point. _____

First-Rate View

Fill in the blanks to show the approximate rate for climbing these famous structures.

Rate

Climbing the Statue of Liberty at about 360 steps in 30 minutes is a rate of _____ steps per minute.

Climbing the Monument to the Great Fire of London at about 300 steps in 30 minutes is a rate of _____ steps per minute.

Climbing the Taipei 101 Tower at about 3,135 steps in 57 minutes is a rate of _____ steps per minute.

The fastest run up the Empire State Building has been about 1,575 steps in 9 minutes. That record rate is _____ steps per minute.

Climbing the Moorish Clock Tower at about 440 steps in 20 minutes is a rate of _____ steps per minute.

Upon completion, add this sticker to your path on the map!

Brain Box

A **rate** is a special kind of ratio that compares measurements of different units. In a **unit rate**, the quantity of the second unit is always 1. To find a unit rate, treat the ratio as a fraction and find an equivalent fraction with a denominator of 1. For example, a ratio of 90 miles in 2 hours is a unit rate of 45 miles per hour: $\frac{90}{2} = \frac{45}{1}$

Level 6 complete!

Add this achievement sticker
to your path...

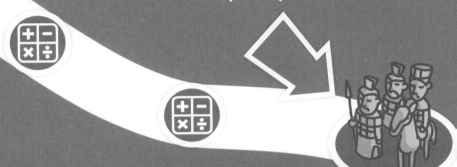

...and move on to

Level 7

on page 110!

Like It Was Yesterday . . .

Think of a time and place in your past that you remember fondly. Close your eyes. What did you see, hear, feel, smell, and taste when you were at that place? List those items.

Writing
Narratives

START
LEVEL
7
HERE!

Upon completion, add this sticker to your path on the map!

What I saw

_____

_____

_____

_____

_____

_____

What I felt

_____

_____

_____

_____

_____

_____

What I heard

_____

_____

_____

_____

_____

_____

What I smelled

_____

_____

_____

_____

_____

_____

What I tasted

_____

_____

_____

_____

_____

_____

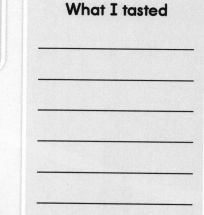

Brain Box

Relevant **sensory details**, such as sights, sounds, feelings, smells, and tastes, help bring a scene to life, so that readers feel like they are there. These may include details about food, weather, nature, objects, people, and animals.

History of Us

Read about early humans. Then fill in the timeline with the correct time period or event.

111

Meet the Hominins

Different species of hominins evolved from apes 5 to 7 million years ago in Africa. Through the years, the various species shared common traits: They walked on two legs, used tools, made fire, and could plan ahead. This allowed them to adapt to many environments. An ice age began 2.5 million years ago, and wild climate swings made it hard for the hominins to survive. Around 200,000 years ago, Homo sapiens evolved from hominins. They would be the only hominin species to survive the Ice Age.

The first successful trek from Africa by modern humans happened 85,000 years ago, when just 200 people crossed the Red Sea. These explorers went on to populate the entire world outside of Africa. (This is why Africa, with a wider base of human ancestors, is the most diverse continent on the planet.) Humans populated Asia first, and then migrated to Australia as early as 60,000 years ago, Western Europe 50,000 years ago, and the Americas 20,000 years ago.

Throughout the Ice Age, humans were hunters and gatherers. At the end of the Ice Age, the climate became more predictable. People began planting the seeds they gathered and taming the animals they hunted. People domesticated goats 12,000 years ago in the Middle East, and 10,000 years ago, squash was being grown in Mexico. Rice paddies were planted in China 6,000 years ago. Farming was perhaps the most important cultural revolution of all time. The steady supply of food allowed large groups of people to live in small areas, setting the stage for civilizations to rise beginning around 5,000 years ago.

BONUS: What conclusions can you draw about an animal's eating habits based on a fossil that shows sharp, pointy teeth today?

Timeline:

- 5 to 7 million years ago — [ ]
- [ ] — Beginning of the Ice Age
- 200,000 years ago — [ ]
- [ ] — First successful trek of modern humans out of Africa
- 60,000 years ago — [ ]
- 50,000 years ago — [ ]
- 20,000 years ago — [ ]
- [ ] — Domestication of goats
- [ ] — Domestication of squash
- [ ] — First rice paddies

Early Humans

Upon completion, add this sticker to your path on the map!

Now add this sticker to your map!

Earth and Human Activity

Upon completion, add this sticker to your path on the map!

Darn Tootin'

Study the chart about sources of greenhouse gas emissions. Then list three actions that can be taken in your home, at school, and by the government to reduce greenhouse gas emissions.

Total U.S. Greenhouse Gas Emissions by Economic Sector

Agriculture: fertilizing, irrigating, tilling, and managing cow manure

Commercial and residential: burning fuel for heating and cooking

Industry: mainly burning fossil fuels for energy to produce raw materials and products

Electricity: burning coal, oil, and natural gas to produce electricity for homes and businesses

Transportation: burning oil to power cars, trucks, airplanes, ships, and trains

9%
12%
30%
21%
26%

Brain Box

The **global temperature** is rising due to an increase of carbon dioxide (a greenhouse gas) in the atmosphere. Carbon dioxide is caused by the burning of fossil fuels. Greenhouse gases are also emitted through agriculture and the clearing of forests. Because of the rise in temperature, drier areas are becoming drier, wetter areas are more flood-prone, and glaciers are melting, resulting in rising sea levels and many hardships for people. Switching to renewable power sources, such as wind, solar, geothermal, hydro, and biofuels, can help reduce greenhouse gas emissions.

Home

_____
_____
_____

School

_____
_____
_____

Local, State, or Federal Government

_____
_____
_____

Tree Talk

Solve the equations.

Trees around buildings in a big city can reduce air-conditioning costs by 30%. How much would that save on a $210 bill?

$$210 \times \frac{30}{100} =$$

Maple tree leaves turn bright colors in the fall. If 80% of the 65 trees on a piece of land are maple trees, how many trees will have bright colors in the fall?

$$65 \times \frac{80}{100} =$$

There are 80 different kinds of mangrove trees, and 75% of them live on coasts between the high- and low-tide lines. How many kinds of mangrove trees fit that category?

Upon completion, add this sticker to your path on the map!

Some research shows that people will spend 12% more in shopping areas that have trees. If you have spent $50 on a shopping trip in an area without trees, how much more will you spend in an area that has trees?

A California coast redwood is the tallest tree in the world, at just under 380 feet tall. The Statue of Liberty is about 80% of its height. How tall is the Statue of Liberty?

Brain Box

A **percent** is a ratio with 100 as the second term— 30% means "30 out of every 100."

Island of the Giants

Read the paragraph about Rapa Nui and the moai.

Around 1,200 miles east of the Pitcairn Islands and 2,300 miles west of Chile lies the most isolated inhabited island on Earth: Rapa Nui, or Easter Island, as it was called by European settlers. It's nearly treeless now, making the moai—giant stone sculptures that inhabit the island—that much more dramatic. When did people first reach this desolate place? And what do the statues mean?

According to oral history, a Polynesian chief, Hotu Matu'a, led a group of settlers in outrigger canoes to the distant island, having heard about it from earlier explorers. Scientists believe Matu'a's group arrived at least 800 years ago, and found the island much different than it is today. It was covered by palms and other vegetation, all of which is now gone. At the time, food was plentiful enough that not everyone had to work the land. A class of workers had begun erecting giant stone statues—some weighing 75 tons and standing 40 feet tall—called moai. They lined the island, facing inward, perhaps to honor the gods or ancestors of the island.

Archaeologists originally thought that the trees were felled to move the statues, but legend has it that the moai "walked" to their designated places. Archaeologists have shown that people could have accomplished this dramatic display by pulling the upright statues along with ropes. So what, then, happened to the trees?

New studies show that the forest ecosystem collapsed for two reasons: First, people cleared some of the forests to make fields for their crops. Second, rats that had traveled in the canoes as stowaways multiplied quickly on the island, finding no natural predators and a smorgasbord of tree seeds. With the seeds eaten, new trees weren't able to replace those that died naturally or were burned. As the trees went, so did the fruits and many of the birds that had relied on the trees for food and shelter. Without protection from the trees, the soil eroded too. Now the people were deprived of the birds they hunted, the fruit they foraged, and the land they farmed—not to mention wood for canoes with which to fish.

Still, the people survived, eating the very rats that overtook the island and engineering gardens that derived nutrients from rocks. Incredibly, the work on the moai continued through the environmental collapse. However, when European settlers arrived on the island, any struggles the people were facing worsened. The population declined due to foreign diseases, and soon construction of the moai stopped altogether. They can still be viewed today—testaments to human ingenuity and resilience.

What is the central idea of the text?

The moai were likely transported upright.

People settled the isolated island of Rapa Nui hundreds of years ago, thriving in good times and surviving through hardships.

Invasive species can be harmful to an ecosystem.

How is the text organized?

Events are described chronologically.

Two ideas are compared and contrasted.

What two reasons are given for the collapse of the island's ecosystem?

_____

_____

List four hardships from the text that the people endured once the ecosystem collapsed.

_____

_____

_____

_____

What can you infer from the text about the first Rapa Nui settlers' seafaring abilities? Support your answer with a fact from the text.

_____

_____

Imagine that you are the chief who has led your people to a new, uninhabited island. List the first five things you would do upon arrival.

_____

_____

_____

_____

_____

Experts have inferred that the moai, because they face the interior of the island, honor ancestors or gods on the island. What could be inferred if they were facing outward?

_____

_____

_____

_____

Reading Informational Texts

Upon completion, add these stickers to your path on the map!

Graphing—
Positive
and
Negative
Numbers

Weather Worldwide

Mark the points above and below 0 on the vertical number line according to the directions below.

Degrees in Fahrenheit

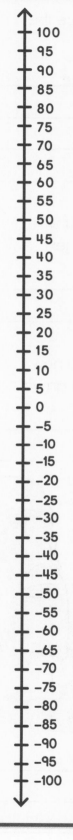

- 100
- 95
- 90
- 85
- 80
- 75
- 70
- 65
- 60
- 55
- 50
- 45
- 40
- 35
- 30
- 25
- 20
- 15
- 10
- 5
- 0
- −5
- −10
- −15
- −20
- −25
- −30
- −35
- −40
- −45
- −50
- −55
- −60
- −65
- −70
- −75
- −80
- −85
- −90
- −95
- −100

The temperature in Phoenix, Arizona, is 95°, hot, and dry. Mark the point in **red**.

The temperature at the North Pole is −5° and foggy. Mark the point in **green**.

The temperature at the South Pole is −65° with blowing snow. Mark the point in **blue**.

The temperature in Kyoto, Japan, is 70° and cloudy. Mark the point in **gray**.

A tornado blew items east and west from a house that is at point 0. Mark the points to the right and left of 0 on the horizontal number line.

Graphing—Positive and Negative Numbers

A boy's bike was found 10 yards west. Mark the point in **purple**.

A bamboo mat was found 18 yards east. Mark the point in yellow.

A flowerpot was found 9 yards east. Mark the point in **pink**.

An embroidered quilt was found 14 yards west. Mark the point in **green**.

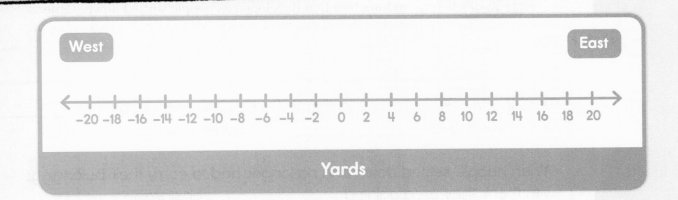

West | East

–20 –18 –16 –14 –12 –10 –8 –6 –4 –2 0 2 4 6 8 10 12 14 16 18 20

Yards

YOU'VE REACHED LEVEL 7'S GATEWAY.

If you have

unlock the gate by adding to your map.

If not, retrace your steps to find the key!

Brain Box

Positive numbers are 1, 2, 3, 4, . . .

Negative numbers are -1, -2, -3, -4, . . .

0 is neither positive nor negative.

On a vertical number line, positive numbers run up from 0 and negative numbers run down from 0.

On a horizontal number line, positive numbers run to the right from 0 and negative numbers run to the left from 0.

Neolithic
Revolution

Upon
completion,
add this
sticker to
your path on
the map!

Revolutionary

Read about artifacts from the Neolithic Revolution. Then fill in the blanks.

Earthenware bowl, China, 5,300 to 4,050 years ago

China's Neolithic Revolution took place along the Yellow and Yangzi rivers, two of the earliest birthplaces of agriculture. With people settling down, farming instead of hunting and gathering, and accumulating more food and personal items, painted pottery was used for storage. This bowl was made by coiling clay into place and then smoothing the surface with scrapers. It was then fired and painted.

Plastered skull with shell eyes, Jericho, 9,000 to 7,200 years ago

Jericho is one of the oldest continuously lived-in cities in the world. And it's no wonder: Freshwater springs make it a welcome oasis in the desert. Many Neolithic artifacts have been found here, including human skulls belonging to men, women, and children, plastered over and painted to resemble living heads. These could have been symbols used for ancestor worship or reminders of loved ones lost.

Stonehenge, England, 5,000 years ago

Henges—circular structures built into the earth—became common in Britain during the Neolithic Revolution, though their exact purpose is unknown. They may have been celestial calendars, religious temples, or burial grounds. Stonehenge, impressive for its size and structure, is an example of the architecture that developed as people settled down. Experts believe that it was built communally over hundreds of years.

The Neolithic Revolution is the shift 11,500 to 4,000 years ago from _____ and gathering to _____ and settlement.

When people settled down and no longer had to carry their belongings with them, they used painted _____ for storage.

Like photographs today, plastered skulls may have been reminders of _____ who had died.

Stonehenge is an example of Neolithic _____ , which is a result of people settling down.

CONGRATULATIONS!
You completed all of your social studies quests!
You earned:

Arabian Nights

Read the facts. Then write a five-sentence paragraph about *The Thousand and One Nights* in your own words with a topic sentence, three supporting details, and a concluding statement.

The Thousand and One Nights, also known as *The Arabian Nights*, is a collection of stories from the Middle East and South Asia.

It dates from at least the early 900s CE.

The stories were collected over hundreds of years by writers and scholars.

The stories are part of a frame story, during which all the other stories are told.

The frame story is that a woman tells a story each night to an evil king (her husband), saving the ending for the following night so that the king keeps her alive another day to hear it.

The king is so intrigued by the stories that he spares his wife's life each night.

Some of the most well-known stories in the West, including "Aladdin's Wonderful Lamp" and "Ali Baba and the Forty Thieves," were added to later editions of the collection.

The Thousand and One Nights was widely translated and read.

It influenced and inspired European and British authors, including Geoffrey Chaucer, who wrote the classic frame story *The Canterbury Tales*.

Informative Writing

Upon completion, add this sticker to your path on the map!

_____

_____

_____

_____

_____

_____

_____

_____

Brain Box

An **informative paragraph** should have a topic sentence and **supporting details**, which may include relevant facts, details, definitions, and examples.

Writing
Explanatory
Texts

So, What Do You Know?

Choose one of the topics or write your own topic. Then brainstorm important steps and relevant information for an explanatory essay.

How to Make a Friend

How to Write a Story

How to Build a Bird House

How to Tread Water

How to Pack a Picnic

How to _____

Brainstorm relevant steps and information: _____
_____

Materials needed: _____
_____

Estimated Amount of Time Needed: _____
_____

First Step: _____
_____

Second Step: _____
_____

Third Step: _____
_____

Other Steps: _____
_____
_____

Brain Box

An **explanatory text** explains a process or procedure. When writing an explanatory essay, it's important to include complete and accurate information in a logical order so the reader can successfully complete the task.

Write your explanatory essay.

Introduction paragraph (State why the reader might want to complete the activity, how you learned to do the activity, and how difficult or easy the activity is.)

_____

_____

_____

_____

_____

Writing
Explanatory
Texts

Main paragraph (Explain how to do the activity. If the activity is complicated, you may need to break this up into two paragraphs.)

_____

_____

_____

_____

_____

_____

_____

_____

_____

_____

_____

Upon
completion,
add these
stickers to
your path on
the map!

Diagram (Draw a diagram that will help the reader understand the instructions.)

Concluding paragraph (Encourage the reader to test his or her knowledge by completing the activity.)

_____

_____

_____

Expand Your Horizons

Expand the number by writing it as a multiplication problem.

$4^3 =$

$15^4 =$

$16^2 =$

$9^6 =$

$3^5 =$

Write each expanded number as a single number with an exponent.

$13 × 13 =$

$43 × 43 × 43 =$

$8 × 8 × 8 × 8 × 8 =$

$6 × 6 × 6 × 6 × 6 × 6 × 6 =$

Find the value of each number.

$12^2 =$

$10^5 =$

$15^4 =$

$2^6 =$

$11^3 =$

$1^{10} =$

Is 3^5 equal to 5^3? Explain.

Brain Box

$3^4 = 3 × 3 × 3 × 3 = 81$

Here 4 is the exponent, 3 is the base. To find the value of a number with an exponent, multiply the base by itself as many times as the exponent shows. Read the exponent 2 as "squared." Read the exponent 3 as "cubed."

Cross-Number Puzzle

Evaluate the expressions to complete the cross-number puzzle. (HINT: Follow the order of operations.)

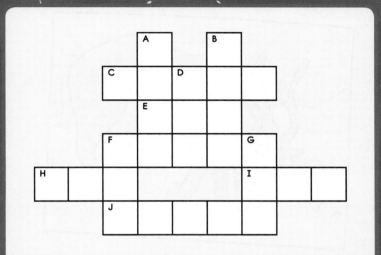

Expressions with Exponents

Upon completion, add these stickers to your path on the map!

Across

C $6^6 - 3^3 =$

E $16^2 - (2 \times 4^2) =$

F $2 \times 6^5 =$

H $2^8 =$

I $(4^3 + 7) \times 12 =$

J $9 \times 10^4 =$

Down

A $10^3 + 5^4 =$

B $3 \times 20^2 + (9 \times 5) =$

D $5^2 \times 5^2 =$

F $217 - 3 \times 2^4 =$

G $(5 + 3^2) \times 20 =$

CONGRATULATIONS!
You completed all of your math quests!
You earned:

Ecosystems

Boreal for Real

You are a photographer on assignment in a boreal forest. Draw a line from each photo to the correct caption.

Coniferous trees survive the cold, dry winters of the boreal forest in many ways. Snow slides off the trees because of their conical shapes. A waxy coating on the leaves prevents water loss through transpiration. (Typically, trees release water through the pores of their leaves, but the coating on the pine needles stops the release of the water.) And, helpful during months of scarce sunlight, the trees conserve energy by keeping their needles for several years.

Omnivores are both primary and secondary consumers.

Brain Box

An **ecosystem** is a group of various organisms that interact with one another and their environment. It includes **decomposers**, organisms that break down dead organisms into nutrients for the soil; **producers**, plants and fungi that provide food to animals; **primary consumers**, animals that only eat plants and fungi; and **secondary consumers**, animals that eat primary consumers. An organism can fall into more than one category.

125

Ecosystems

Animals adapt to the snowy environment by molting in the late summer so that their coats change from brown to white.

Primary consumers are food for secondary consumers.

Upon completion, add these stickers to your path on the map!

Lichens such as the moss eaten by reindeer and caribou are both decomposers and producers. They digest dead organisms, breaking them down into nutrients for the soil. They also provide food for consumers of the forest.

CONGRATULATIONS!
You completed all of your science quests! You earned:

Creative
Writing

Upon
completion,
add this
sticker to
your path on
the map!

Fortunate Smiles

Finish the "Fortunately, Unfortunately" story.
The "Fortunately" lines should tell something
good that happens to the character. The
"Unfortunately" lines should tell something
bad that happens.

Princess Gwendolyn was trying on her mother's priceless royal
crown when it tumbled off her head, out the window, and into
the moat.

Fortunately, Gwendolyn knew how to swim, so she dove in to
retrieve it.

Unfortunately, _____

_____

Fortunately, _____

_____

Unfortunately, _____

_____

Fortunately, _____

_____

Unfortunately, _____

_____

Fortunately, _____

Brain Box

A **plot** consists of the main
events of the story. Typically,
these follow a pattern of
ups and downs for the main
characters. As the characters
respond to the ups and downs,
they grow, change, and come
to understand themselves better.

CONGRATULATIONS!
You completed
all of your English
language arts
quests! You
earned:

Quest complete!

Add this achievement sticker to your path…

QUEST complete! Welcome to 6th grade!

…and turn to the next page for your Summer Brainiac Award!

Summer Brainiac Award!

You have completed your entire Summer Brain Quest! Woo-hoo! Congratulations! That's quite an achievement.

Write your name on the line and cut out the award certificate. Show your friends. Hang it on your wall! You're a certified Summer Brainiac!

Summer Brainiac Award

Presented to:

_____

for successfully completing the learning journey in

SUMMER BRAIN QUEST®: BETWEEN GRADES 5 & 6

Outside Quests

Outside
Quests

This is not just a workbook—it's an exotic expedition, a flight through foreign lands, a way to enjoy the summer sunshine, and so much more! Summer is the perfect time to explore the great outdoors. Use the Outside Quests to make your next sunny day more fun than ever—and earn an achievement sticker.

Outside
Quests

Now add this sticker to your map!

Level 2 — Rock, Paper, Empire!

With sidewalk chalk, draw 10 one-foot squares in a row. You and a friend will stand on opposite ends of the row. The square each of you stands on represents your home country. The other squares are countries you are trying to conquer. Play life-size rock, paper, scissors. For rock, curl up in a ball. For paper, stand with your legs and arms straight. For scissors, lift one leg to your knee and hold your arms up in a V. If you win the first challenge, move forward one square to conquer a country. If you lose, stay still. The person who conquers most countries wins the empire.

Level 4A — Prepositional Race

With a partner, build a prepositional obstacle course in your yard or at a park. Choose 5 of the following words:

above	beside	over	under
across	between	past	to
around	onto	through	down

Designate an obstacle to go with each word. It may be a structure that is already there or one you create. Then time yourself and your friend to see who completes the obstacle course the fastest.

Example: Run to the tree. Climb over a branch. Jump down. Crawl through the tunnel. Jump onto the rock.

Now add this sticker to your map!

Outside
Quests

Level 5C Volcano!

Make a chemical reaction with household products. Go outside and build a volcano with clay, mud, or rocks with a small cup inside. Pour a tablespoon of baking soda into the cup. Add a tablespoon of dish soap and a few drops of red food coloring (this just makes the eruption colorful and bubbly; it's not necessary for the actual reaction). Finally, add a cup of vinegar, and watch the volcano erupt. The equation for the reaction is $C_2H_4O_2$ (the acetic acid in the vinegar) + $NaHCO_3$ (baking soda) = $NaC_2H_3O_2$ + H_2O + CO_2 (the gas that makes bubbles!). This is an acid-base reaction. You can try the same experiment with another acidic liquid—lemon juice.

Now add this sticker to your map!

Level 5A Jumping Powers of 10

Go outdoors with a partner and sidewalk chalk. Write any 3-digit number on a hard surface with about 1 foot between the digits. Stand between any of the digits—you are the decimal point! Then your partner tells you to jump 1, 2, or 3 places to the right or the left. Jump the amount of places and say what number you made. Write it down. See how many numbers you can make without repeating a number. Remember to add 0s to fill empty places. For example, if the number is 245 and you start between the 4 and 5 and jump 3 places left, you have made 0.0245. If you jump 3 places to the right, you have made 24,500. Next, it's your partner's turn. Who can make more unique numbers?

Now add this sticker to your map!

Now add
this sticker
to your
map!

(Level 5B) Name That Adventure

Go on a journey named after you! Find a partner and a notepad, and walk around your neighborhood. Search for objects that begin with each letter in your names, and write each word. Then take turns using the collection of words to make up a story about an adventure you're on. Strange foods? Ferocious creatures? Hostile weather? You decide!

Now add
this sticker
to your
map!

(Level 5A) Olympians!

The Olympics originated in Ancient Greece more than 2,700 years ago. The original events were footraces, but wrestling, chariot racing, and more were added later. Host a mini Olympics with friends or family members. Make up four events in which everyone will compete. They can be serious (a sprint, long jump, baseball throw, and gymnastics routine, for instance) or silly (egg toss, three-legged race, tug-of-war, and balancing race, for example). Then divide people into two or more countries. (If you only have two people, you will each be a country.) Establish a schedule, rules, courses, and scoring system. Then compete to determine the Olympic champion!

Outside
Quests

Level 6
Sidewalk Calculations

Take some chalk outdoors to a sidewalk.
Draw the face of a calculator: 16 connected squares in 4 rows of 4. Write the digits 0, 1, 2, 3, 4, 5, 6, 7, 8, 9, and the symbols +, -, ×, ÷, and =, one in each box. In the 16th box, write a small 2 for exponent 2. Choose a number, and then hop on the numbers and symbols as if it were a calculator, to show how you can use the operations to make that number. See how many different ways you can make the number. For example, to make 16, you could:

- hop from 4 to + to 4 to + to 4 to + to 4 to = (4 + 4 + 4 + 4 = 16)
- hop from 4 to × to 4 to = (4 × 4 = 16)
- hop from 4 to exponent 2 to = (4^2 = 16)
- hop from 3 to × to 3 to + to 7 to = (3 × 3 + 7 = 16)

Now add this sticker to your map!

Level 7
Survivor: Your Neighborhood

Track a nonthreatening wild animal in your neighborhood, like a squirrel, bird, or an insect. Observe features and behaviors that help this animal avoid threats and acquire food. Also note any features or qualities that are helpful or unhelpful in the modern world. For example, you might notice deer find the most to eat on the edge of forests and in more open habitats, like fields. The current way people use and live on land creates a lot of these types of areas, and thus many spaces where deer and people can interact or clash. When you get home, list traits that are helpful, not helpful, or helpful in some ways but not others.

Now add this sticker to your map!

Key Quests

Key Quests

Research is a process of gaining knowledge by gathering new information. When you find the information you're looking for, it's like finding a key that unlocks a door to a whole new world.

To retrieve a key, choose one of the following topics or write your own. Then write a research question. (A good research question cannot be answered with a simple yes or no—you will need to look for answers in a few reliable sources.) Lastly, paraphrase three facts from your source that you learned.

Key Quests

KEY QUEST

TOPICS

Aboriginal culture
Ancient Egyptian inventions
Famous activists outside of the US
Battles in Ancient Greece
Extinct languages of Asia
Animals of the Amazon

_____

Research question: _____

_____

Fact #1 _____

_____

Fact #2 _____

_____

Fact #3 _____

_____

Now add this sticker to your map!

KEY QUEST

TOPICS

Survival skills for extreme weather
Polar animals
Effects of solar energy
Writers of the Constitution
Yetis: mythical or real?
The Silk Road

_____

Research question: _____

_____

Fact #1 _____

_____

Fact #2 _____

_____

Fact #3 _____

_____

Now add this sticker to your map!

Answer Key

(For pages not included in this section,
answers will vary.)

LEVEL 1

page 10

Yesterday, my sister and I reached Giza. Hurray! We are now pyramid builders. Our job is to move stone blocks from the bottom of the ramp to the top, all to honor our great pharaoh! Our task is simple, but it's neither easy nor foolproof. During the heat of the afternoon, another team lost its grip on a block. The block rolled over a worker's arm, crushing it. Horrible! Doctors came immediately, thank Ra!

By the end of the day, my sister and I were famished. Back home, we are used to small portions of rice and fish at mealtime. Imagine our surprise when heaping plates of pork, goat, and mutton were passed around the table. Yum! After dinner, I tried listening to my new friends' stories, but I couldn't keep my eyes open. Instead, I fell asleep on the hard ground under the stars.

(Letters marked above text: C, I, P, C, I, I, P, P, C, P, P, I, P)

page 11
Answers will vary. Sample:

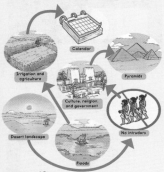

page 12
C
Ca, O

page 13
4,326,185
329,608
7,007,070
60,894
0.659
5.463
1.07
17.088

page 14
have studied
have wanted
hadn't brought
had created
had taken
had escaped
have asked
will have returned
BONUS: Answers will vary.

page 15
kinetic
potential
both
kinetic
potential

page 16
20   23
23.2   23.17
$9.00; $10.00
$40.00; $38.50
$20.00; $17.00
$1.80
$5.80
BONUS: 6.485, 6.486, 6.487, 6.488, 6.489, 6.490, 6.491, 6.492, 6.493, 6.494

LEVEL 2

page 18

- The streets were laid out in a grid.
- People had good personal hygiene.
- The society was peaceful, as buried bodies do not show signs of violence.
- They had a system of writing.
- Kids played games.

BONUS: Answers will vary.

page 19
and
either
but
whether
Not only
neither

page 20
$50 - 5 \times (2 + 1) = 35$
$(50 - 5) \times 2 + 1 = 91$
$12 \times 3 - (2 + 1) = 33$
$12 \times (3 - 2) + 1 = 13$
$6 \div 3 \times (2 + 4) = 12$
$6 \div (3 \times 2) + 4 = 5$

page 21
$6 \times 294 - 55$; $1,709
$498 - 2 \times 149$; $200 more
$2 \times (945 + 1,054)$; 3,998 feet
$(10 \times 60 + 30) - (3 \times 60 + 30)$; 420 minutes
$(2 \times 45) + (2 \times 60) - (3 \times 60)$; 30 minutes
BONUS: $[(5 \times 189) - 50] \div 5 = 179$; Each person pays $179.

page 22

A swimmer kicks and water splashes. — 3
A feather sails and falls to the ground because of air friction and gravity. — 1
It takes two people to push a stalled car two miles per hour. — 2
An ant carries a seed many times its body weight three inches per second. — 2
A tumbleweed rolls until it hits a cactus. — 1

BONUS: force

page 23
the Mediterranean Sea
Yes.
Answers will vary. Sample: Romans could travel by sea to various locations in the empire.
Answers will vary. Sample: The Romans based their gods on the Greek gods.

page 24
Don't count your chickens before they hatch.
The best defense is a good offense.
Never look a gift horse in the mouth.
The time to repair the roof is when the sun is shining.
Don't put all your eggs in one basket.

page 27

	Athens	Sparta
	False	True
	True	True
	False	True
	True	True
	False	True

Answers will vary.
BONUS: Answers will vary.

page 28

Year	0	1	2	3	4	5
Doubtful Designer's Tower	0	1	2	3	4	5
Poor Planner's Tower	0	2	4	6	8	10
Bad Builder's Tower	0	6	12	18	24	30

twice or 2 times
2, 4, 6, 8, 10, …
6 times
6, 12, 18, 24, 30, …
3 times
3, 6, 9, 12, 15, …

LEVEL 3

page 30

koala	both	Tasmanian devil
single cub	sharp	multiple cubs
ample sleep	teeth	competitive behavior
herbivore	produce milk	carnivore
	sharp claws	

page 31
New South Wales
Tasmania
east coast
Western Australia
an open bay
BONUS: It is warmer on average in the Northern Territory than in Tasmania.

page 32

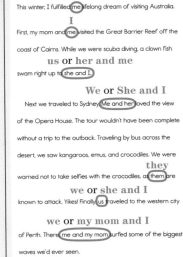

This winter, I fulfilled **me** [my] lifelong dream of visiting Australia.

First, my mom and **me** [I] visited the Great Barrier Reef off the coast of Cairns. While we were scuba diving, a clown fish swam right up to **she and I.** [us or her and me]

Next we traveled to Sydney. **Me and her** [We or She and I] loved the view of the Opera House. The tour wouldn't have been complete without a trip to the outback. Traveling by bus across the desert, we saw kangaroos, emus, and crocodiles. We were warned not to take selfies with the crocodiles, as **them** [they] are known to attack. Yikes! Finally **us** [we or she and I] traveled to the western city of Perth. There **me and my mom** [we or my mom and I] surfed some of the biggest waves we'd ever seen.

I absolutely loved Australia!

page 33

As a reader grows more confident, he or she chooses more challenging books. / As readers grow more confident, they choose more challenging books.

A babysitter must be able to multitask, or else he or she will quickly become overwhelmed. / Babysitters must be able to multitask, or else they will quickly become overwhelmed.

A basketball player usually perfects his or her shooting outside of team practice. / Basketball players usually perfect their shooting outside of team practice.

If someone from camp calls, tell him or her I just stepped out for a minute. / If people from camp call, tell them I just stepped out for a minute.

BONUS: Answers will vary.

page 34

389 × 4 = 1,436
429 × 51 = 21,879
74 × 16 = 1,184
726 × 3 = 2,178
39 × 48 = 1,872
371 × 88 = 32,648

page 35

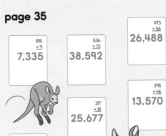

815 × 9 = 7,335
536 × 72 = 38,592
473 × 56 = 26,488
317 × 81 = 25,677
295 × 46 = 13,570
64 × 92 = 5,888
864 × 13 = 11,232

pages 36–37

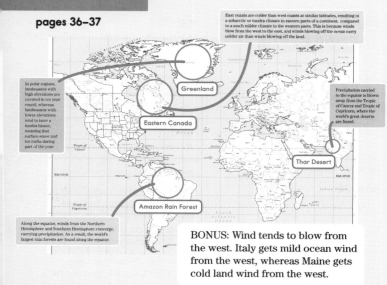

In polar regions, landmasses with high elevations are covered in ice year round, whereas landmasses with lower elevations tend to have a tundra biome, meaning that surface snow and ice melts during part of the year.

Greenland

Eastern Canada

Amazon Rain Forest

Thar Desert

East coasts are colder than west coasts at similar latitudes, resulting in a subarctic or tundra climate in eastern parts of a continent, compared to a much milder climate in the western parts. This is because winds blow from the west to the east, and winds blowing off the ocean carry milder air than winds blowing off the land.

Precipitation carried away from the equator is blown to the Tropic of Cancer and Tropic of Capricorn, where the world's great deserts are found.

Along the equator, winds from the Northern Hemisphere and Southern Hemisphere converge, carrying precipitation. As a result, the world's largest rain forests are found along the equator.

BONUS: Wind tends to blow from the west. Italy gets mild ocean wind from the west, whereas Maine gets cold land wind from the west.

pages 38–39

$3\overline{)343}$	$9\overline{)675}$	$4\overline{)924}$	$23\overline{)5,129}$	$18\overline{)6,948}$	$32\overline{)7,264}$
114 r1	75	231	223	386	227

$6\overline{)5,298}$	$3\overline{)3,702}$	$5\overline{)3,239}$	$83\overline{)2,241}$	$61\overline{)2,135}$	$87\overline{)3,828}$
883	1,234	647 r4	27	35	44

BONUS: 52 costumes

page 40

$19\overline{)722}$	$36\overline{)2,270}$	$48\overline{)2,160}$	$92\overline{)4,692}$	$67\overline{)1,685}$
38	63 r2	45	51	25 r10

$36 \times 63 \div 2 = $ 2,270

$38 \times 19 = 722$

$45 \times 48 = $ 2,160

$25 \times 67 + 10 = $ 1,685

$92 \times 51 = $ 4,692

page 41

What looks like a rat, is as big as a cat, and is totally lovible? It's the quokka, a marsupial living in Australia. On the mainland, invasive species such as foxes have hunted the quokka to lower numbers, but they're still prevalent on surrounding islands. Because the animals are furry and cute (they have the appearance of always smiling), visitors have taken a shine to the quokka. In turn, the quokkas have become quite comfortible around people, and will even pose for selfies with them! #Adorible! Experts say that while taking a selfie is harmless, other behaviors are undesirible. Visitors should refrain from touching the animals (however huggible they appear). And feeding a quokka is an especially terrable idea. The adaptible quokka will readily eat people food, but it gets stuck in the animal's teeth, making the quokka vulnerible to infection. So remember, it's okay to say *cheese* with a quokka. Just don't feed it cheese afterwards.

lovable
comfortable
adorable
undesirable

huggable
terrible
adaptable
vulnerable

LEVEL 4A

page 44

5.118 Mexico	>	0.236 Germany

5.118 Mexico	<	6.7 South America

0.157 Austria	>	0.123 Sweden

0.123 Sweden	>	0.118 Italy

0.4 Southern U.S.	<	0.461 India

page 45

0.504 Peru	<	0.551 Turkey

0.504 Peru	>	0.492 North Africa

2.4 Eastern U.S.	>	2.25 Southeast Asia

0.492 North Africa	>	0.118 Italy

1.26 Thailand	>	1.142 Kenya

0.5 < 0.504 or 0.504 > 0.5

The Eastern U.S. beetle, which is 2.4 inches

The South American beetle, which is 6.7 inches

page 46

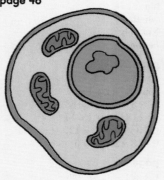

page 47

Parents tried to arrange marriages with young men and women of equal or higher status.

If young people from the lower or middle class proved themselves to be talented or remarkable in some way, they could "marry up" in status.

Upper-class children were formally trained in etiquette.

Summer was the busiest time for Pacific Northwest people, as they fished, gathered, and preserved food for winter.

People traveled in small groups to various home sites in the summer but reunited in their villages in the winter.

During winter, high-class people often focused on social obligations and art, having slaves do their day-to-day labor.

Art from the Pacific Northwest, as seen on sculptures such as totem poles, was bold and stylized.

Pacific Northwest people used the plentiful wood available to build huge homes, buildings, and dugout canoes.

page 48

helpful
neither helpful nor harmful
both helpful and harmful

page 49

bat
bear
park
bluff
overlook
rock
wind
story

page 50

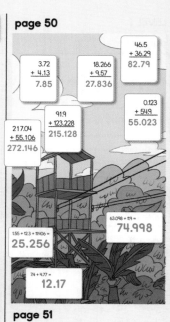

$3.72 + 4.13 = 7.85$

$18.266 + 9.57 = 27.836$

$46.5 + 36.29 = 82.79$

$91.9 + 123.228 = 215.128$

$0.123 + 54.9 = 55.023$

$217.04 + 55.106 = 272.146$

$1.55 + 12.3 + 11.406 = 25.256$

$63.098 + 11.9 = 74.998$

$7.14 + 4.77 = 12.17$

page 51

$8.6 - 4.2 = 4.4$

$0.321 - 0.16 = 0.161$

$45.7 - 10.49 = 35.21$

$73.44 - 31.18 = 42.26$

$99.7524 - 0.852 = 98.9004$

$9.2 - 1.52 = 7.68$

$55.43 - 4.33 = 51.1$

$71.05 - 1.6 = 69.45$

$6.285 - 2.08 = 4.205$

pages 52–53

a butterfly

You remind me of my childhood.

They were friends.

Answers will vary. Sample: She was kind and cared about creatures like butterflies.

Answers will vary. Sample: Like a hunter

Bittersweet

The loveliest memories are the most fragile.

page 54

LEVEL 4B

page 57
ab
phobia
Acr
am
anthropo
botan
scribe
camp
BONUS: Answers will vary.

page 59
✓ The scientist fanned herself with the fallen palm **leaf** ~~frond~~.
✗ The Amazon **River** ~~creek~~ is the largest river in the world by volume.
✗ The toucan lives in the rain forest **canopy** ~~umbrella~~, the layer of forest in which leaves and branches create continuous shade.
✓ Tree **trunks** ~~stems~~ in the rain forest tend to be tall and bare, except for a collection of branches and leaves at the top.
✗ Parrots use their strong jaws to break open shells and eat the **seeds** ~~nuts~~ inside.

BONUS: Answers will vary.
Samples: Two definitions of the word "net" may include:
an open-meshed fabric that is twisted, knotted, or woven together at regular intervals; an entrapping device or situation; a group of communications stations operating under unified control

page 60
$0.7 \times 0.8 = 0.56$
$0.813 \times 0.2 = 0.1626$
$9.57 \times 0.11 = 1.0527$
$8.9 \times 0.25 = 2.225$
$0.21 \times 0.22 = 0.0462$
$13.6 \times 0.47 = 6.392$
$29.25 \times 8 = 234$
$45.4 \times 0.3 = 13.62$
BONUS: 525 deer

LEVEL 5B

page 62
walking slowly
dirty
wound from a sword
unsteady
knocked
an expert in matters of taste
nice location on the bay
many customers
resting place

page 63
Make a solar oven to bake cookies

The oven must get very hot. Therefore, the solar oven must absorb and retain as much heat from the sun as possible.

She covers the inside of a pizza box with foil and places plastic wrap over the box where the cookies are baking.

Not well enough—the cookies are raw inside.

She insulates the box with foam, covers the foam with foil-lined cardboard, and uses glass instead of plastic wrap.

page 64
$\frac{1}{2} = \frac{1 \times 3}{2 \times 3} = \frac{3}{6}$ | $\frac{1}{3} = \frac{1 \times 2}{3 \times 2} = \frac{2}{6}$
$\frac{1}{3} = \frac{1 \times 5}{3 \times 5} = \frac{5}{15}$ | $\frac{2}{5} = \frac{2 \times 3}{5 \times 3} = \frac{6}{15}$
$\frac{3}{4} = \frac{3 \times 12}{4 \times 12} = \frac{36}{48}$ | $\frac{5}{12} = \frac{5 \times 4}{12 \times 4} = \frac{20}{48}$
$\frac{1}{2} = \frac{1 \times 8}{2 \times 8} = \frac{8}{16}$ | $\frac{3}{8} = \frac{3 \times 2}{8 \times 2} = \frac{6}{16}$
$\frac{5}{12} = \frac{5 \times 6}{12 \times 6} = \frac{30}{72}$ | $\frac{1}{6} = \frac{1 \times 12}{6 \times 12} = \frac{12}{72}$
$\frac{3}{4} = \frac{3 \times 6}{4 \times 6} = \frac{18}{24}$ | $\frac{5}{6} = \frac{5 \times 4}{6 \times 4} = \frac{20}{24}$
yes
no

page 65
Crossword: illness, inva..., gunpowder, conquerors, compass, m a..., hor...

BONUS: Answers will vary.
Samples:
A natural disaster in the homeland
Overcrowding in the homeland
Disagreement or persecution in the homeland
Seeking better food sources
Seeking riches
A religious quest
Adventure

page 66
$\frac{1}{2} + \frac{3}{4} = \frac{2}{4} + \frac{3}{4} = \frac{5}{4} = 1\frac{1}{4}$
$\frac{1}{2} + \frac{2}{3} = \frac{3}{6} + \frac{4}{6} = \frac{7}{6} = 1\frac{1}{6}$
$\frac{5}{8} + \frac{1}{4} = \frac{5}{8} + \frac{2}{8} = \frac{7}{8}$
$\frac{9}{16} + \frac{3}{4} = \frac{9}{16} + \frac{12}{16} = \frac{21}{16} = 1\frac{5}{16}$
$\frac{1}{2} + \frac{3}{12} = \frac{6}{12} + \frac{3}{12} = \frac{9}{12} = \frac{3}{4}$
$\frac{15}{16} + \frac{1}{4} = \frac{15}{16} + \frac{4}{16} = \frac{19}{16} = 1\frac{3}{16}$
$\frac{9}{10} + \frac{1}{5} = \frac{9}{10} + \frac{2}{10} = \frac{11}{10} = 1\frac{1}{10}$
$\frac{5}{6} + \frac{3}{4} = \frac{10}{12} + \frac{9}{12} = \frac{19}{12} = 1\frac{7}{12}$

page 67
$1\frac{1}{3} + 1\frac{3}{5} = 1\frac{5}{15} + 1\frac{9}{15} = 2\frac{14}{15}$
$2\frac{1}{6} + \frac{2}{3} = 2\frac{1}{6} + \frac{4}{6} = 2\frac{5}{6}$
$\frac{9}{10} - \frac{1}{12} = \frac{54}{60} - \frac{5}{60} = \frac{49}{60}$
$2\frac{7}{8} - \frac{3}{4} = 2\frac{7}{8} - \frac{6}{8} = 2\frac{1}{8}$
$1\frac{5}{6} - \frac{3}{4} = 1\frac{10}{12} - \frac{9}{12} = 1\frac{1}{12}$
$2 - \frac{5}{12} = 1\frac{12}{12} - \frac{5}{12} = 1\frac{7}{12}$

page 69
The lotus was so delicious that they stopped caring about going back home
They willingly share their lotus with others.
Answers will vary.
Answers will vary.

page 70
$\frac{2}{3} + \frac{2}{3} + \frac{2}{3} + \frac{2}{3} = \frac{8}{3}$
$\frac{2}{3} = \frac{4}{1} \times \frac{2}{3} = \frac{4 \times 2}{1 \times 3} = \frac{8}{3} = 2\frac{2}{3}$

$5 \times \frac{2}{10} = \frac{10}{10} = 1$ | $3 \times \frac{3}{8} = \frac{9}{8} = 1\frac{1}{8}$ | $4 \times \frac{3}{4} = \frac{12}{4} = 3$
$5 \times \frac{1}{3} = \frac{5}{3} = 1\frac{2}{3}$ | $7 \times \frac{5}{6} = \frac{35}{6} = 5\frac{5}{6}$ | $3 \times \frac{4}{10} = \frac{12}{10} = 1\frac{2}{10} = 1\frac{1}{5}$
$10 \times \frac{1}{5} = \frac{10}{5} = 2$ | $2 \times \frac{7}{12} = \frac{14}{12} = 1\frac{2}{12} = 1\frac{1}{6}$ | $7 \times \frac{2}{5} = \frac{14}{5} = 2\frac{4}{5}$

page 71
$\frac{2}{6}$ or $\frac{1}{3}$
$\frac{1}{2} \times \frac{2}{3} = \frac{1 \times 2}{2 \times 3} = \frac{2}{6} = \frac{1}{3}$

$\frac{3}{8} \times \frac{1}{3} = \frac{3}{24} = \frac{1}{8}$ | $\frac{7}{16} \times \frac{1}{2} = \frac{7}{32}$ | $\frac{4}{10} \times \frac{2}{3} = \frac{8}{30} = \frac{4}{15}$
$\frac{2}{5} \times \frac{1}{4} = \frac{2}{20} = \frac{1}{10}$ | $\frac{1}{6} \times \frac{5}{6} = \frac{5}{36}$ | $\frac{3}{4} \times \frac{3}{8} = \frac{9}{32} = \frac{1}{4}$
$\frac{2}{5} \times \frac{7}{8} = \frac{14}{40} = \frac{7}{20}$ | $\frac{1}{3} \times \frac{1}{4} = \frac{1}{12}$ | $\frac{3}{10} \times \frac{2}{5} = \frac{6}{50} = \frac{3}{25}$

BONUS: 21 miles per hour

page 72
Answers may include: Also, In addition, Moreover, Similarly
Answers may include: For example, For instance
Answers may include: Also, In addition, Moreover, Similarly
Answers may include: Although, Yet, However, On the other hand, In other words

LEVEL 5A

page 74
condensation, transpiration, precipitation, downhill flow, evaporation, crystallization

page 75

Vikings were a seafaring people from Scandinavia who, from 800 to 1100 CE, raided Britain, other parts of Europe, and beyond, and ultimately settled in those lands. The Vikings' motive (is) simple: They desired wealth in the form of stolen riches and captured slaves. Before they set out to pillage distant nations, the Scandinavians had been trading iron and fur with closer European nations. From these trade partners, the Scandinavians (already adept sailors) (learn) how to build better ships. They also learned of the fractured feudal kingdoms in Britain and Europe—easy pickings for the Vikings.

The Vikings' first raids were on monasteries in Britain, which were left unguarded because most warriors left religious institutions alone. But the Vikings (are) not Christians and (have) no respect for such institutions. They soon settled in Scotland and Ireland, launching their attacks and trading enterprises from there. They later came to reside in Europe, Iceland, and Greenland. Eventually, Scandinavia was converted to Christianity, and the Christianized Viking culture (merges) with the cultures of its adopted lands.

was
learned
were
had
merged

page 76

 $\frac{1}{2}$; $\frac{1}{2}$

 $\frac{1}{3}$; $\frac{1}{3}$

$\frac{2}{3}$; $\frac{2}{3}$

 $\frac{3}{2} = 1\frac{1}{2}$; 3 ; $1\frac{1}{2}$

page 77

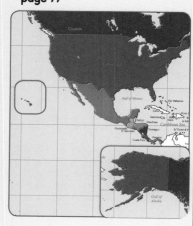

BONUS: Answers will vary. Sample: They share an ancestry from when Australia and South America were connected as part of a larger continent, called Pangaea.

page 78

If 4 pirate cooks divided $\frac{1}{2}$ pound of dried beans equally, how much would each cook get?
$\frac{1}{2} \div 4 = \frac{1}{8}$ pound(s)

After mealtime, there was $\frac{1}{3}$ kilogram of sea biscuits left. If a cook shared the leftovers with the captain equally, how much would each person receive?
$\frac{1}{3} \div 2 = \frac{1}{6}$ kilogram(s)

One-fourth of a gallon of fishbone soup was shared equally among 4 pirates. What was each pirate's share?
$\frac{1}{4} \div 4 = \frac{1}{16}$ gallon(s)

$\frac{1}{25}$

$\frac{1}{16}$

$\frac{1}{18}$

page 79

The chef made 4 pickled-beet pizzas, and equally divided each into eighths. How many slices of pizza did he make?
$4 \div \frac{1}{8} =$ **32** slice(s)

The chef divided 5 gallons of sauerkraut into one-sixth gallon portions. How many portions of sauerkraut were there?
$5 \div \frac{1}{6} =$ **30** portion(s)

Ten pounds of salt pork were divided into shares that were $\frac{1}{4}$ pound each. How many shares were there?
$10 \div \frac{1}{4} =$ **40** share(s)

20
18
70

pages 80–81

sleepy and stupid

Answers will vary. Sample: dazed

She is prone to panic.

Answers will vary. Sample: She is caring/thoughtful/conscientious.

Answers will vary. Sample: She is curious/brave/adventurous/open-minded.

Faced with a world that doesn't make sense, Alice learns just how brave and capable she really is.

Third-person limited

BONUS: Answers will vary.

page 82

$3 \times \frac{7}{10} = \frac{21}{10} = 2\frac{1}{10}$	$2\frac{1}{10}$ kilometers
$15\frac{3}{4} - 6\frac{1}{2} = 9\frac{1}{4}$	$9\frac{1}{4}$ kilometers
$4 \div 3 = \frac{4}{3} = 1\frac{1}{3}$	$1\frac{1}{3}$ sandwiches

page 83

$8 \div \frac{1}{2} = 16$	16 times
$5 \times \frac{5}{6} = \frac{25}{6} = 4\frac{1}{6}$	$4\frac{1}{6}$ hours
$\frac{1}{10} \div 2 = \frac{1}{20}$	$\frac{1}{20}$ kilogram
$\frac{1}{3} \times 2 = \frac{2}{3}$	$\frac{2}{3}$ cups

BONUS: $\frac{1}{2} \div 3 = \frac{1}{6}$; $\frac{1}{6}$ pound

page 84

species
morphology
genes
traits
evolved
breeding
mutation
domestication
generations
BONUS: A pet is an individual animal raised by a human for companionship; a domesticated animal is a species that over many generations has been bred to live among humans for a variety of reasons.

LEVEL 5C

page 86

Bottom layer = $6 \times 6 = 36$
There are 9 layers, so $9 \times 36 = 324$
324 ft³
3 feet = 1 yard, therefore bottom layer = $2 \times 2 = 4$
There are 3 layers, so $3 \times 4 = 12$
12 yd³
864 ft³
32 yd³

pages 88–89

Mercury and Mars
Mercury
Neptune
It's closer to the sun. (Also, its extreme greenhouse gases make it better at trapping heat than Earth.)
It's one of the closest planets to Earth, but is farther away from the sun, so it is not too hot to visit.

page 91

The main idea of the text is follow safety rules when ice fishing.

Answers will vary. Samples:
Ice must be a certain depth for walking and driving.
Many fishermen have lost their lives due to a safety mistake.
If you fall through the ice, crawl out and roll to safety.
indicates

experienced
Ice on a lake must be 8 inches deep for a group walking on a lake.
"Ice Fishing Safety Rules" states problems and solutions, whereas "Ice Cold Fishing!" describes events chronologically.

LEVEL 6

page 94

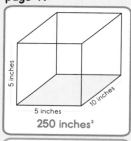
250 inches³

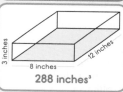
288 inches³

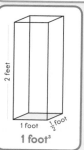
1 foot³

125 inches³

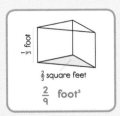

40 square inches
80 inches³

⅔ square feet
$\frac{2}{9}$ foot³

Page 95

l = 17 units w = 3 units h = 4 units **(O)** V = __204__ units³	l = 8 units w = 5 units h = 8 units **(W)** V = __320__ units³	l = 15 units w = 10 units h = 2 units **(N)** V = __300__ units³
l = 3 units w = 3 units h = 19 units **(A)** V = __171__ units³	l = 8 units w = 8 units h = 8 units **(P)** V = __512__ units³	l = 20 units w = 4 units h = 8 units **(G)** V = __640__ units³
	l = 22 units w = 18 units h = 1 unit **(L)** V = __396__ units³	l = 6 units w = 6 units h = 9 units **(Y)** V = __324__ units³

POLY-GON AWAY

page 97

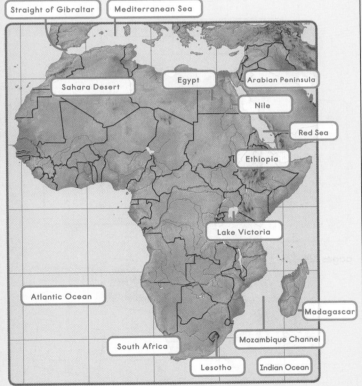

Straight of Gibraltar · Mediterranean Sea · Sahara Desert · Egypt · Arabian Peninsula · Nile · Red Sea · Ethiopia · Lake Victoria · Atlantic Ocean · Madagascar · Mozambique Channel · South Africa · Lesotho · Indian Ocean

BONUS: The Sahara Desert farmers migrated to wetter areas, spreading the practice of raising animals.

pages 98–99

W	R
W	RW
R	R
R	RW

BONUS: Answers will vary.
Samples: Plants need nutrients in soil to grow. Palms need sand deposited by the ocean in which to grow.

page 102

6:4; 6, 4
8:4; 8, 4
3:6; 3, 6
1:6; 1, 6
1:3; 1, 3
3:14; 3, 14

page 105

Answers will vary.
BONUS: There is frequent flooding in the region.

page 106

(2, 5)
(4, 10)
(6, 15)
(8, 20)

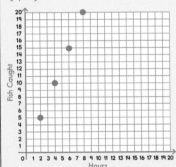

page 107

(4, 5)
(3, 9)
(9, 7)
(7, 1)

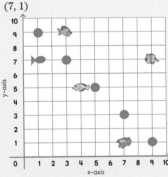

The order of the numbers is important because if you change the order, it is a different location on the graph.
Each point is 2 units to the right and 2 units down from the one before.
BONUS: (9, 1)

page 108

12
10
55
175
22

LEVEL 7

page 111

Hominins evolved from apes
2.5 million years ago
Homo sapiens evolved from hominids
85,000 years ago
Homo sapiens reached Australia
Homo sapiens reached Western Europe
Homo sapiens reached the Americas
12,000 years ago
10,000 years ago
6,000 years ago
BONUS: The animal probably ate meat, like other sharp- and pointy-toothed animals today.

page 113

$63
52 trees
$80 \times \frac{75}{100} = 60$ trees
$\$50 \times \frac{12}{100} = \$6$
$380 \times \frac{80}{100} = 304$ feet

pages 114–115

People settled the isolated island of Rapa Nui hundreds of years ago, thriving in good times and surviving through hardships.

Events are described chronologically.

Invasive rats ate the tree seeds, and people burned vegetation for their crops.

The soil eroded, making farming difficult.
Fruit was now unavailable.
Several birds that had been a food source disappeared.
There was no wood for canoes.

Because the Rapa Nui settlers' were able to travel at least 1,200 miles across the Pacific, they must have been expert seafarers.

Answers will vary.

Answers will vary. Samples: They were protecting the island, they were built to scare others away, they were honoring ancestors/gods away from the island.

142

page 116

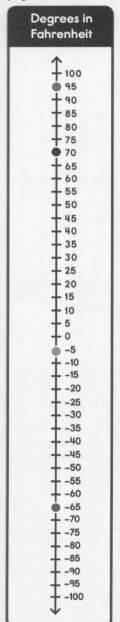

Degrees in Fahrenheit

page 117

West / East

Yards

page 118

hunting; farming or agriculture
pottery
loved ones
architecture

page 122

Expand the number by writing it as a multiplication problem.

$4^3 = 4 \times 4 \times 4$ $15^4 = 15 \times 15 \times 15 \times 15$
$16^2 = 16 \times 16$ $9^6 = 9\times9\times9\times9\times9\times9$
$3^5 = 3 \times 3 \times 3 \times 3 \times 3$

Find the value of each number.

$12^2 = 144$
$10^5 = 100{,}000$
$15^4 = 50{,}625$
$2^6 = 64$
$11^3 = 1{,}331$
$1^{10} = 1$

Write each expanded number as a single number with an exponent.

$13 \times 13 = 13^2$
$43 \times 43 \times 43 = 43^3$
$8 \times 8 \times 8 \times 8 \times 8 = 8^5$
$6 \times 6 \times 6 \times 6 \times 6 \times 6 \times 6 = 6^7$

Is 3^5 equal to 5^3? Explain. No. $3^5 = 243$ and $5^3 = 125$.

page 123

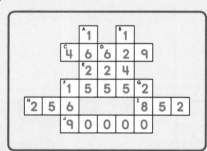

Across

C $6^6 - 3^3 = 46{,}629$
E $16^2 - (2 \times 4^2) = 224$
F $2 \times 6^5 = 15{,}552$
H $2^8 = 256$
I $(4^3 + 7) \times 12 = 852$
J $9 \times 10^4 = 90{,}000$

Down

A $10^3 + 5^4 = 1{,}625$
B $3 \times 20^2 + (9 \times 5) = 1{,}245$
D $5^2 \times 5^2 = 625$
F $217 - 3 \times 2^4 = 169$
G $(5 + 3^2) \times 20 = 280$

pages 124–125

Summer Brain Quest Extras

Stay smart all summer long with these Summer Brain Quest Extras! In this section you'll find:

Summer Brain Quest Reading List

A book can take you anywhere—and summer is a great time to go on a reading adventure! Use the Summer Brain Quest Reading List to help you start the next chapter of your quest!

Summer Brain Quest Mini Deck

Cut out the cards and make your own Summer Brain Quest Mini Deck. Play by yourself or with a friend.

Summer Brain Quest Reading List

We recommend reading at least 15 to 30 minutes each day. Read to yourself or aloud. You can also read aloud with a friend or family member and discuss the book. Here are some questions to get you started:

- Was the book a nonfiction (informational) or fiction (story/narrative) text?

- Who or what was the book about?

- What was the setting of the story (where did it take place)?

- Was there a main character? Who was it? Describe the character.

- Was there a problem in the story? What was it? How was it solved?

- Were there any themes in the story? What were they? How do you know?

- Were there any lessons in the story? What were they? How do you know?

- Why do you think the author wrote the book?

Jump-start your reading adventure by visiting your local library or bookstore and checking out the following books. Track which ones you've read, and write your own review! Would you recommend this book to a friend? If so, which friend would you recommend this book to, and why?

Fiction

Among the Hidden (Shadow Children Series, No. 1), by Margaret Peterson Haddix

In the dystopian future, the Population Police limits families to having only two children. Luke, a third child, lives in the attic of his parents' farm in complete isolation until he meets a girl just like him. Jen wants to march on Washington, but Luke is wary. What is he willing to risk for his freedom?

DATE STARTED: _____   DATE FINISHED: _____

MY REVIEW: _____

_____

_____

Bindi Babes, by Narinder Dhami

Amber, Geena, and Jazz are three popular sisters who rule their school. Though outwardly confident, at home they're dealing with their mother's recent death and the arrival of their nosy aunt from India. The girls devise a plan to get auntie to leave . . . by marrying her off!

DATE STARTED: _____   DATE FINISHED: _____

MY REVIEW: _____

_____

_____

Blackbird Fly, by Erin Entrada Kelly

After her dad died when she was little, Apple and her mom moved from the Philippines to Louisiana. Here, Apple's classmates tease her for being Asian, but her mother complains that she has become "too American." Apple takes refuge in music, determined to buy a guitar and blaze her own lyrical trail.

DATE STARTED: _____   DATE FINISHED: _____

MY REVIEW: _____

_____

_____

In the Year of the Boar and Jackie Robinson, by Bette Bao Lord

It's 1945, and self-named Shirley Temple Wong has just sailed all the way from China to Brooklyn, New York. Shirley doesn't speak English, and none of her classmates look like her. But when Shirley learns about Jackie Robinson, a black baseball player, everything changes.

DATE STARTED: _____   DATE FINISHED: _____

MY REVIEW: _____

_____

_____

A Long Walk to Water: Based on a True Story, by Linda Sue Park

Salva is an 11-year-old boy in 1985 when he is separated from his family by the war in Sudan and forced to wander through the desert in search of water and shelter. Nya is a young Sudanese girl in 2008 who walks hours every day to fetch water from a pond. Watch their stories of survival weave together.

DATE STARTED: _____   DATE FINISHED: _____

MY REVIEW: _____

_____

_____

The Mysterious Benedict Society, written by Trenton Lee Stewart, illustrated by Carson Ellis

Lured in by a mysterious newspaper ad and recruited by the odd Mr. Benedict after passing his series of tests, Reynie, Sticky, Kate, and Constance are sent on a secret mission: to go undercover at the Learning Institute for the Very Enlightened and pass the most difficult test of all.

DATE STARTED: _____   DATE FINISHED: _____

MY REVIEW: _____

_____

_____

The Night Gardener, written by Jonathan Auxier, illustrated by Patrick Arrasmith

Orphaned siblings Molly and Kip flee to England, where they work as servants at the Windsor estate. The house is eerie, its inhabitants shape-shifting and deeply evil. Can Molly and Kip stop this ancient curse, once and for all?

DATE STARTED: _____ DATE FINISHED: _____

MY REVIEW: _____

_____

_____

Okay for Now, by Gary D. Schmidt

Doug Swieteck's new life in tiny Marysville, New York, is rough. Can he rescue himself? When all the odds are against him, he learns invaluable lessons about love, creativity, and how to survive small-town life.

DATE STARTED: _____ DATE FINISHED: _____

MY REVIEW: _____

_____

_____

One Crazy Summer, by Rita Williams-Garcia

In the summer of 1968, sisters Delphine, Vonetta, and Fern travel from New York to stay with their mother, who left them seven years ago for the more radical lifestyle of California. They'd expected trips to Disneyland, but the girls are instead sent to a Black Panther day camp, and start to get a taste for another world.

DATE STARTED: _____ DATE FINISHED: _____

MY REVIEW: _____

_____

_____

Then Again, Maybe I Won't, by Judy Blume

Ever since moving to a bigger house, 13-year-old Tony has found the people around him to be dishonest. His mom is acting differently, his dad hushes problems with gifts, and his next-door neighbor is shoplifting. On top of everything else, he's starting to feel new things for his other neighbor, Lisa. When did he get so many problems?

DATE STARTED: _____ DATE FINISHED: _____

MY REVIEW: _____

_____

_____

Nonfiction

Aliens Are Coming! The True Account of the 1938* War of the Worlds *Radio Broadcast, written and illustrated by Meghan McCarthy

In 1938, the radio broadcast of a science-fiction novel about an alien invasion was taken as truth by many Americans and caused mass hysteria. Read about this crazy event!

DATE STARTED: _____ DATE FINISHED: _____

MY REVIEW: _____

_____

_____

The Emperor's Silent Army: Terracotta Warriors of Ancient China, by Jane O'Connor

In 1974, thousands of life-size terracotta warrior statues were found in northern China. Unearth this archaeological dig and the inspiration behind the 7,500 figures, which are one of the wonders of the world.

DATE STARTED: _____ DATE FINISHED: _____

MY REVIEW: _____

_____

_____

Freedom Walkers: The Story of the Montgomery Bus Boycott, by Russell Freedman

On December 1, 1955, Rosa Park's refusal to move to the back of the bus launched a city-wide boycott of the bus system that resulted in its desegregation. Read about the brave people who brought about change during the civil rights movement.

DATE STARTED: _____ DATE FINISHED: _____

MY REVIEW: _____

_____

_____

Girls Think of Everything: Stories of Ingenious Inventions by Women, written by Catherine Thimmesh, illustrated by Melissa Sweet

Women have been creating revolutionary innovations since the beginning of time, from ancient weaving to modern solar-heated houses. And where would we be without chocolate chip cookies?

DATE STARTED: _____ **DATE FINISHED:** _____

MY REVIEW: _____

_____

_____

Guinea Pig Scientists: Bold Self-Experimenters in Science and Medicine, written by Leslie Dendy and Mel Boring, illustrated by C. B. Morgan

Thanks to scientists who first tested their inventions on themselves, we have everything from radiation therapy to heart catheters. These scientists might have infected themselves with deadly diseases, so don't try this at home!

DATE STARTED: _____ **DATE FINISHED:** _____

MY REVIEW: _____

_____

_____

Life on Earth—and Beyond: An Astrobiologist's Quest, by Pamela S. Turner

Dr. Chris McKay studies the conditions necessary to sustain life. Learn about his travels from Antarctica to North Africa in search of extreme environments that mimic what it might be like in outer space!

DATE STARTED: _____ **DATE FINISHED:** _____

MY REVIEW: _____

_____

_____

Parrots Over Puerto Rico, written by Susan L. Roth and Cindy Trumbore, illustrated by Susan L. Roth

Compassion for Puerto Rican parrots is historical—scientists have found centuries-old materials used to mend injured wings! Follow this side-by-side history of vibrant Puerto Rico and the parrots that have populated it for the last 2,000 years.

DATE STARTED: _____   DATE FINISHED: _____

MY REVIEW: _____

_____

_____

Tutankhamun: The Mystery of the Boy King, by Zahi Hawass

Learn about the exquisite lives of the great pharaohs across 3,000 years of ancient Egyptian history through photographs of real artifacts, from royal eye makeup to pet cat sarcophagi!

DATE STARTED: _____   DATE FINISHED: _____

MY REVIEW: _____

_____

_____

What the World Eats, written by Faith D'Aluisio, photographed by Peter Menzel

Sit down to dinner with families around the world!

DATE STARTED: _____   DATE FINISHED: _____

MY REVIEW: _____

_____

_____

Who Wins?: 100 Historical Figures Go Head-to-Head and You Decide the Winner!, written by Clay Swartz, illustrated by Tom Booth

Who would win in a lightsaber duel: Charles Dickens or Mother Teresa? Read their bios, then mix and match 100 historical figures in 50 competitive categories, from Ping-Pong to climbing Mount Everest!

DATE STARTED: _____   DATE FINISHED: _____

MY REVIEW: _____

_____

_____

And don't stop here!
There's a whole world
to discover. All you
need is a book!

Summer Brain Quest Mini Deck

QUESTIONS

 What is the standard form of nine million, nine hundred fifty-two thousand, sixty?

 Find the coordinating conjunction in this sentence: "The climate is hot and dry."

 In a chemical reaction, does the total number of atoms change or stay the same?

In what Egyptian city is the Great Pyramid located?

QUESTIONS

 An Empire State Building T-shirt costs $14.79. You paid by giving the clerk the amount to the nearest tenth. How much did you hand the clerk?

 Is the verb in the past perfect, present perfect, or future perfect tense? "By then I will have run 1,000 miles."

 What number is missing? $K_2O + H_2O = \_KOH$

Which came first, the Peloponnesian War in Ancient Greece or the fall of Rome?

QUESTIONS

 A bus tour lasted $2\frac{3}{4}$ hours, and there were three 20-minute stops. How many minutes were you actually on the bus?

 Find the correlative conjunctions (two words): "Either James forgot his key, or he is still home."

 When a gymnast flips, is it an example of potential or kinetic energy?

 What Roman god is most similar to Zeus?

QUESTIONS

 King Kong climbs $\frac{2}{3}$ of the way up a building, takes a break, and then climbs another $\frac{1}{4}$ of the way up. How far up the building is King King?

Who is the hero of *The Odyssey*?

 According to Newton's first law, objects in motion tend to _____ in motion.

 At what age did Spartan boys begin military training?

ANSWERS

 $14.80

 future perfect

 2

 the Peloponnesian War

ANSWERS

 9,952,060

 and

 stay the same

 Giza

ANSWERS

 $\frac{11}{12}$ of the way

 Odysseus

 stay

 7

ANSWERS

 105 minutes

 either, or

 kinetic

 Jupiter

QUESTIONS

 There are 45 floats in a Mardi Gras parade. If 12 people are on each float, what is the total number of people on the floats?

 What is incorrect in this sentence: "My mom threw the football to my brother and I"?

 True or false: All marsupials are mammals.

 Where are the following located: River Murray, Great Victoria Desert, and Perth?

QUESTIONS

 A total of 1,216 people attended a square dance festival. If everyone joined a dance in groups of four, how many groups were there?

 What should replace "their"? "A swimmer must race even if their goggles fill with water."

 Where in the cell is an organism's entire DNA sequence located?

 What entire continent is also the world's largest desert?

QUESTIONS

 Which is smaller, an insect that is 0.504 inches long or one that is 0.054 inches long?

 Does the Latin root "hibern" mean warm or wintry?

 Genes are codes for building what?

 Is the Tropic of Cancer located in the Southern or Northern Hemisphere?

QUESTIONS

 18 children caught and released 126 butterflies. How many butterflies did each student catch if each student caught an equal amount?

 Complete the proverb: Let sleeping dogs _____.

 Evolution occurs slowly through gene _____.

 The Middle Ages began with the fall of what empire?

158

ANSWERS

 304

 his or her

 the nucleus

 Antarctica

ANSWERS

 540

 "I" should be "me."

 true

 Australia

ANSWERS

 7

 lie

 mutations

 the Roman Empire

ANSWERS

 0.054

 wintry

 proteins

 Northern

QUESTIONS

 You go on two amusement park rides. One is 56.25 seconds long. The other is 104.9 seconds long. How long are the two rides together?

 Is the following a simile or metaphor: "Kansas is as flat as a pancake"?

 Which is not a fossil fuel: coal, oil, sunshine?

 What was the capital of the Byzantine Empire?

QUESTIONS

 A hiker glimpsed the Loch Ness monster for 3.18 seconds. How many seconds less than 1 minute is that?

 What is the transitional phrase in this sentence: "In other words, the new swimming pool won't open until July"?

 Is condensation the process of a gas becoming a liquid or a solid?

 Which of these did the Mayans **not** use: a 365-day calendar, a writing system, glittery paint, wheel and axle?

QUESTIONS

 How many decimal places are there in the product of 35.3 and 2.16?

 Is the struggle between two characters or forces the conflict or the theme of a story?

 Which planet is closest to the sun?

 Which came first, the Age of Exploration or the American Revolution?

QUESTIONS

 The Sphinx gave an explorer this question: "What is the product of 2 and the sum of 0.22 and 2.22?" Find the answer.

 Is the following a compound or complex sentence: "When I think of grits, I think of my grandmother's kitchen"?

 Is Mars smaller or larger than Earth?

 Where did the Vikings originally live?

ANSWERS

 56.82 seconds

 in other words

 liquid

 wheel and axle

ANSWERS

 161.15 seconds

 simile

 sunshine

 Constantinople (modern-day Istanbul)

ANSWERS

 4.88

 complex

 smaller

 Scandinavia

ANSWERS

 3

 conflict

 Mercury

 the Age of Exploration

Level 1

START

Level 2

Level 4A

Level 4B

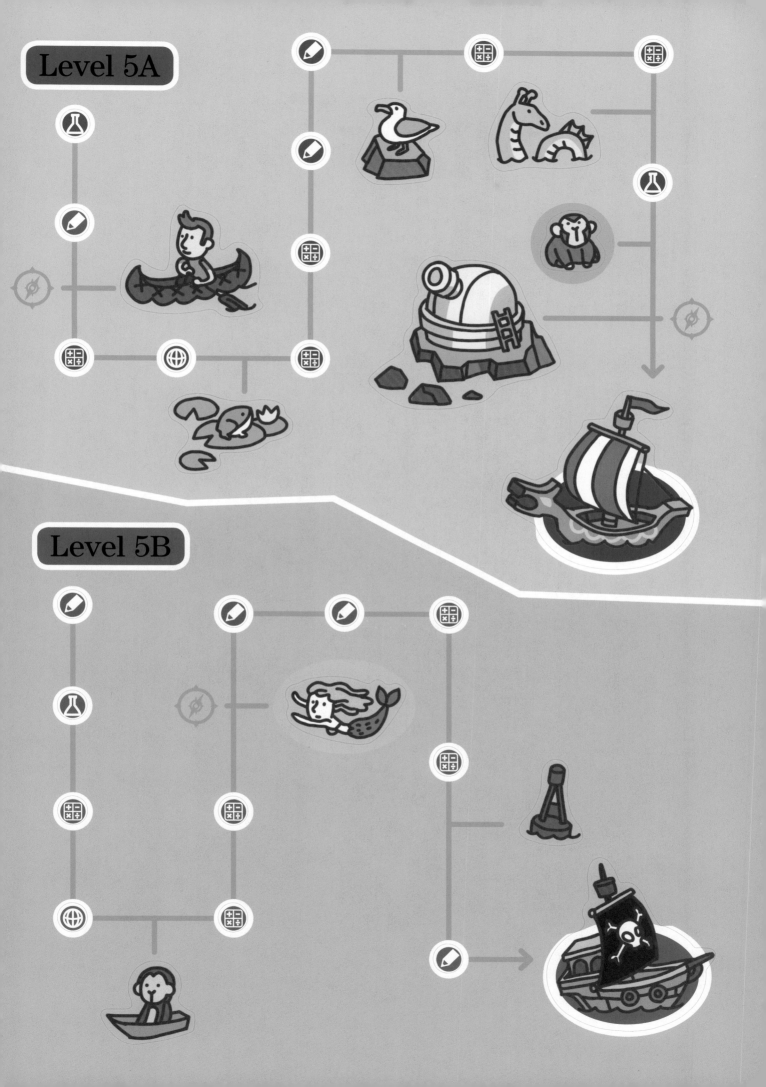

Level 5A

Level 5B

Level 6

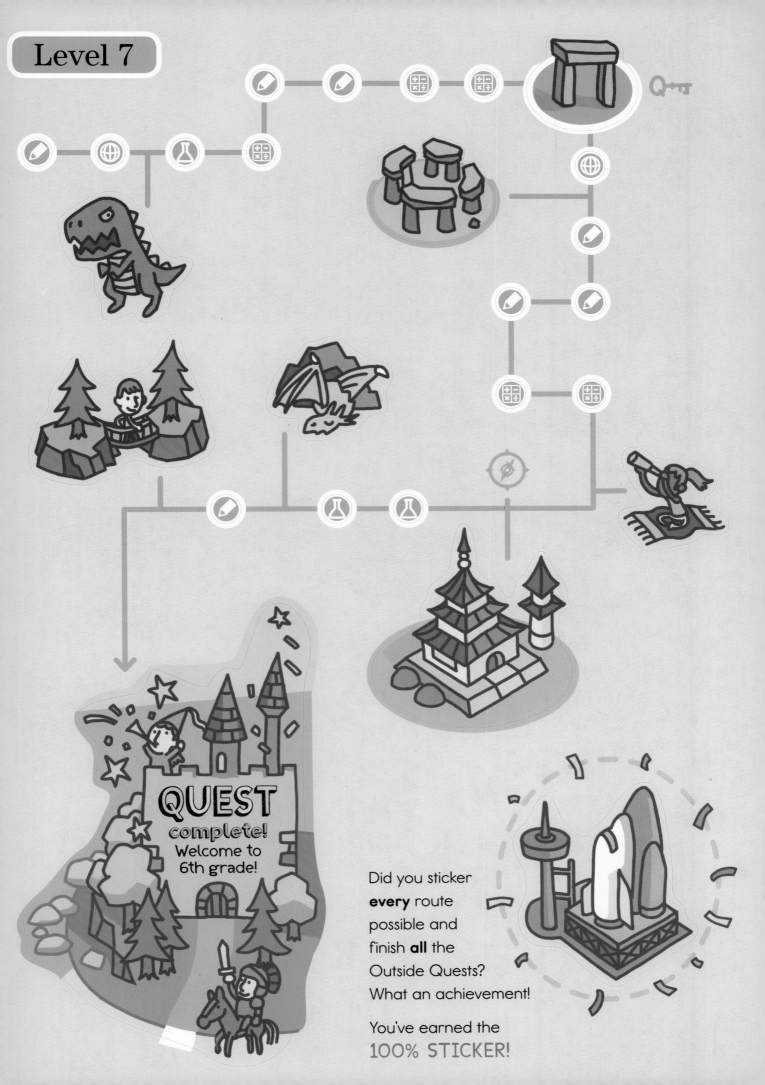

Level 7

QUEST complete!
Welcome to 6th grade!

Did you sticker **every** route possible and finish **all** the Outside Quests? What an achievement!

You've earned the 100% STICKER!

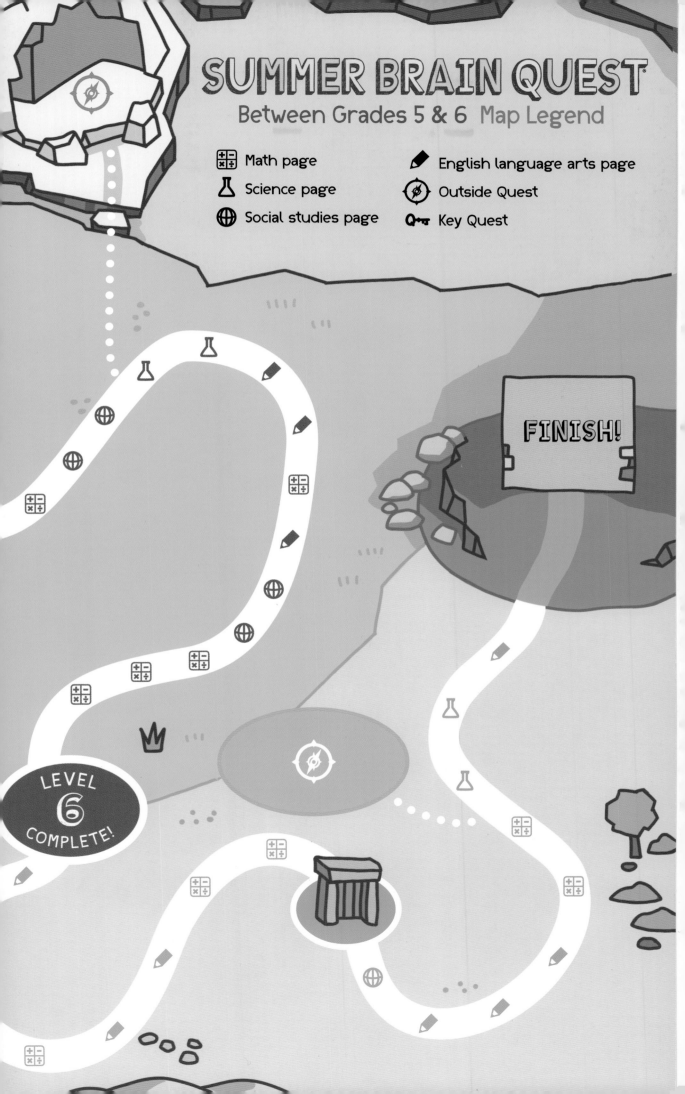

SUMMER BRAIN QUEST

Between Grades 5 & 6 Map Legend

⊞ Math page

⚗ Science page

🌐 Social studies page

✏ English language arts page

◎ Outside Quest

⚷ Key Quest

FINISH!

LEVEL 6 COMPLETE!

KEY QUEST

LEVEL 5C COMPLETE!

LEVEL 5A COMPLETE!

LEVEL 5B COMPLETE!

LEVEL 3 COMPLETE!

LEVEL 4B COMPLETE!